AFRICA
ON WHEELS

Sunset through the acacias in East Africa.

AFRICA
ON WHEELS

A
SCROUNGER'S
GUIDE
TO
MOTORING
IN
AFRICA

john j byrne

© 1973 John J Byrne

ISBN # 0-87799-032-8
LCC # 73-76418

All text and captions in this book are set in Times Roman.
All photos are by the author.
Line drawings are by Randall De Leeuw.

Map of Africa courtesy of Hammond Inc. © 10387

Editor: Michael Cook
Cover and book design: Randall De Leeuw

Published by Haessner Publishing, Inc.
Newfoundland, New Jersey 07435

Printed in the United States of America

CONTENTS

PROLOGUE

Ngorongoro Crater, in northern Tanzania, is a truly awesome chunk of scenery. You stand on the long veranda of the rustic Ngorongoro Crater Lodge, overhanging the crater itself, at about 8,000 feet above sea level. Through an occasional wisp of early morning cloud, you can see into the crater, hundreds of feet below. The saucer of land at bottom is a brilliant Kelly green, dotted with the almost indistinguishable figures of wildebeeste, zebra, and perhaps a prowling lion. In the foreground and slightly to the right of center, as if placed by a meticulous artist, is the lake—shimmering yet placid, an irregular cerulean blotch in all that green. One side of the lake is edged in bright pink, in a sort of amorphous band adhering to the shoreline—consisting of thousands of close-packed flamingos.

This garden of tranquility is happily situated within a day's drive of East Africa's most fabulous attractions. 155 miles to the northeast is Mount Kilimanjaro, all 19,340 feet of her, craggy and snow-shouldered, there for the climbing. On the road to Kilimanjaro, just 37 miles off, lies Lake Manyara National Park, a thin strip of dense vegetation and plentiful game, bounded on one side by lovely Lake Manyara, and on the other by a sheer rock escarpment, rising almost vertically into the heavens. Manyara is the home of the renowned sleeping lions, who lie sprawled about in trees, high above the swarms of tsetse flies at ground level, to the great delight of tourists and photographers.

A scant few miles to the northwest is Olduvai Gorge, rugged and barren seeming, one of the cradles of ancient man. It was here that the late Dr. L.S.B. Leakey discovered *Zinjanthropus* and *Homo habilis,* two of the oldest known predecessors of modern man.

The author and passenger Boyd McBride on the Moroccan coast

East Africa's most sought after tourist sight—lions on a kill.

Just past Olduvai lies Serengeti National Park, the last remaining bastion of free roving game herds in existence. Vast herds of wildebeeste, gazelles, and zebra migrate from spot to spot, ever in search of water and fresh fodder, trailed by their inevitable attendants—the lions, jackals, hyenas, and vultures that prey on the young, the old, the slow, and the sick. In a single morning at Serengeti, we watched and mingled with uncounted thousands of migrating wildebeeste; ran to earth a cheetah, the world's fastest, but rather shortwinded animal; observed a pride of lions on their wildebeeste kill, tawny muzzles stained with blood, glutting themselves against a leaner tomorrow; photographed the king of beasts, a male lion, basking in the sun, from a distance of about ten feet; and watched a pride of lions at play in the shade, grooming one another lazily and playing with their cubs. By noon, we had seen so much wildlife that our minds foundered, unable to assimilate more. Sated, we headed back for another breathtaking look at Ngorongoro.

There are two very different approaches toward achieving the spectacle of East Africa. As always, the simplest is the most direct: fly to Nairobi, rent a Land Rover, and drive south 172 well paved miles to Arusha, situated more or less midway be-

Often obscured by mist and clouds, Kilimanjaro floats wraithlike above a native hut in Northern Tanzania.

tween Kilimanjaro and Lake Manyara. Take the wife and kids, some sleeping bags, plenty of money, and enjoy East Africa in complete safety and comfort. Too easy? Prefer a touch more adventure? Well, you might try it the way I did it: take the ferry from Spain to the North Moroccan coast and head south through the Atlas Mountains, 3500 miles of Sahara Desert, and the still primitive, all but impenetrable Congo, thousands of hard, but gratifying miles through the untouched grandeur that is primitive Africa.

If you happen to be the kind of nut who likes to do everything the hard way, this book will tell you how to travel clear across the African continent by motor vehicle, with little danger and minimal expense. If you prefer things a little tamer, you will learn where you can tour on paved roads, which areas have safe food and sanitary water, in short, how to tour in comfort. In either case, it can cost you less than you'd spend to stay at home

But first, let me tell you about that day in Adrar, where the paved road came to an abrupt end. You have seen Africa at her winsomest; it is only fair that you also see her at her toughest.

YES YOU CAN

We rolled easily into Adrar on a smooth, paved highway, that passed between endless mountains of fine, copper-hued sand and empty wastes of rock and hardpan. According to our Michelin map of North and West Africa, the pavement ended here.

Adrar is a sleepy, little outpost in central Algeria, inhabited by perhaps 50 to 100 souls. It is surrounded by desert, and consists primarily of a single-story, fort-like building, constructed in the form of a huge square. The whole thing conjures up visions of *Beau Geste,* heightened by the fact that the air is filled with tiny grains of abrasive sand, driven by the relentless Sahara wind.

You may not simply drive through Adrar, but are required to stop and obtain an "autorization de voyage" to proceed south. Word is then radioed ahead as each group leaves, so that help can be sent if they should fail to show up at the next town. Shortly before noon, we stopped at the Douane (Customs), which, in typically African fashion, wasted half an hour of our time before referring us to the Chef de Police, who in turn blew 45 minutes before taking us to the Prefecture. The Prefect was just closing for lunch, and suggested that we return at 3:00. At 3:00, he kept us waiting until 4:30, before telling us that it was too late to start out that day and that we should come back at 8:00 in the morning. Such is travel in Africa.

We invested two dinars each in a do-it-yourself shower (you pour water over yourself from a number 10 can) in an unbelievably filthy Arab "bain." We then retired to the town's one and only hotel for a few bottles of tepid Algerian beer at a buck a throw. Things weren't exactly what you'd call looking up.

The leader of our first camel caravan, on the Sahara in central Algeria.

Contrary to popular belief, desert scenery is varied . . .

Surprisingly, we rolled out of town at about 9:45 the next morning, authorizations clutched in our hot, little hands, on one of the most wretched roads I had ever encountered.

There were two carloads of us: myself and two Canadian students in a Volkswagen camper; and two couples in a Land Rover piloted by an American ex-chemist and one-time movie producer named Ed Everts. We were to thank God many times over, in the days to come, for that Land Rover.

It was decided that the VW would lead the way, so the Land Rover could pull us out after (not "if", "after") we got stuck. About a quarter mile out of town, we stopped on a relatively hard patch, and waited for the Rover.

"Ed, are you sure this is the right road?" I asked, practically praying for a negative response.

"Are you kidding? There's only one road in and one road out," explained Ed patiently. "There's no place for another road to go."

I waved my hand in disbelief at the bleak expanse of desert ahead. It was bisected by two severely washboarded, foot-deep ruts, half filled with drifting sand, and was punctuated solely by an oil-drum marker about every two miles. We didn't know it yet, but those oil drums were a real luxury.

. . . and fascinating.

"But it can't go on like this for the next 1,500 miles," I protested hopelessly. "It's all I can do not to get stuck in the road."

This little problem was overcome by driving outside the road, but parallel to it. Needless to say, this created certain difficulties. First, you must keep your speed up to at least 40 m.p.h. in a two-wheel-drive vehicle, both to get through the soft places without bogging down, and to stay in third or fourth gear to conserve petrol. Then, you have to miss: soft patches that will get you stuck; sharp rocks that cut your tires; axle-busting bumps and holes; teeth-rattling washboard; and any "dead end" that will force you to stop and back up (stopping gets you stuck). All this without losing sight of the road, mind you.

The day rapidly degenerated into an endless series of last second, mind-boggling decisions—to miss that soft spot, while avoiding those rocks, without losing the road—at 45 m.p.h. That first day, we stuck the VW three times.

That night, too exhausted to move or speak, I curled up under an eiderdown quilt (it wasn't really that cold), assumed the fetal position, and, quivering uncontrollably, lapsed into a cataleptic trance.

By the end of the second day, I pretty well had the hang of it. After the third day, I got up in the morning looking forward to it. I loved it.

PROS AND CONS:

The disadvantages involved in a cross-continent tour of Africa are legion. A considerable investment in a suitable vehicle must be made, which might be a total loss if you break an axle miles from the nearest settlement. The desert is littered with stripped-out hulks that didn't quite make it. Then there are the tools and equipment you'll have to assemble, the expense, and four to eight months of your time as well. You'll encounter considerable discomfort and frustration. Days, even weeks without a shower, time wasted waiting for visas, intransigent border officials, swarms of tsetse flies, and . . . well, you get the idea.

There are, of course, fantastic rewards: some of the world's most incomparable scenery, the crisp clarity of a starlit desert night, the chance to meet some of the most primitive—and fascinating—peoples on earth, and the solid feeling of accomplishment and comradeship when you've successfully bulled your way through the Congo, or across the Sahara.

During January to August of 1971, I drove from Africa's northern coast, at Tangier, to her southernmost point, near Cape Town, then 1,000 miles back north up the other coast. With a few memorable exceptions, I reveled in each and every minute of it.

I was a thirty-five-year-old lawyer, not a trained mechanic or otherwise specially qualified. The entire 25,000 miles, including 1,544 miles of desert track, was driven in a two-wheel-drive vehicle, with a single spare tire and little in the way of special equipment. Approximate cost, exclusive of travel to Europe and back: $2,000, just under $10 per day.

If I did it, so can you, if you are determined, and have the time, a little money, and the ability to take care of yourself and your vehicle. You need only to follow the first rule of success in writing, sales, or any other endeavor—quit sitting around thinking and talking about it; do it.

You can start by reading the rest of this book.

PICK YOUR
PARTNERS

You would think that passengers being given the free use of a $3,000 vehicular home to cross Africa would be grateful, appreciative, and cooperative in all matters affecting the vehicle and its use, right? Wrong!

I carried one hitchhiker who insisted on putting his muddy boots all over my upholstery. One day, as we bounced across the Sahara, a bag of my small belongings fell out of the overhead space where it had been stored, and landed in the center of the floor. Busy wrestling with the steering wheel, I asked this sterling character to please stuff my things back into the overhead. "They'll just fall out again," he demurred, and sat doing absolutely nothing, while my possessions slid about the floor.

I carried two strong, healthy teenagers, who refused to help me change oil or repair a bent suspension part. They would sit beside the road smoking and watching me fix flats. This continued until I threatened to let them walk across the Congo, after which they reluctantly went through the motions.

On two separate occasions, I spent days on end muttering neurotically to myself because I couldn't get along with a passenger, and couldn't quite bring myself to throw him out, miles from any real civilization, and travel on alone.

In all fairness, I did have the pleasure of traveling with two or three gentlemen, who cheerfully joined in to help me change points and plugs, or repair a puncture, without being asked.

Moral: get straight right from the start just what your passengers will be expected to contribute in the way of work as well as money. Your choice of traveling companions may well be the most important decision you make.

TAKE 'EM OR LEAVE 'EM:

To start with, don't overcrowd. Three or perhaps four people living in a small, confined space for several months are more than enough. Two are sufficient. The more passengers you carry, the more food, clothing, water, and even petrol will have to be lugged along. Extra passengers do, however, reduce the expense per person and add manpower for digging out and pushing (assuming, of course, that you can get them to do any work).

Try to pick people you can get along with. You'll be virtually married to whomever you choose for the duration. This is not as easy as it sounds. For openers, just try to find anyone, anyone at all, who has six months and $2,000 to kill.

Select people who have the time and money to spend, so you won't be left alone in mid-desert, as I was.

Take companions you can trust in an emergency. Your life could literally depend on your partner's coolness and responsibility under stress.

Look for at least one companion who speaks French. French-speaking African officials, having learned by observing real, live Frenchmen, are haughty and disdainful toward those whose Francais is halting or nonexistent. Fluent, or even passable French will solve innumerable border problems.

Be sure that someone in your party is a fair to middlin' amateur mechanic. Whether you have to abandon your vehicle in mid-trek may well depend on your ability to jury rig a fanbelt out of rope, or stop a gas leak with chewing gum. Ed Everts and his wife Debbie (who in some unaccountable fashion acquired the joint nickname, "Captain Deb and Superboot") went so far as to complete the maintenance school at the Land Rover factory in England.

CARAVAN UP:

In an unprecedented display of good sense, the officials at Adrar require all travelers to "caravan up" with at least one other vehicle. This is the only safe, sensible mode of crossing the desert. Do it whether you are forced to or not. Should you suffer a serious mechanical breakdown or run short of fuel or water, the presence or absence of a second car can make the difference between a truly dangerous situation and a future after-dinner story. Ideally, join up with some capable, well equipped companions in a four-wheel-drive vehicle; but in any event join up with someone.

THE WIFE?

By all means, make it a family project. In our group, there were two or three women at all times; they not only managed to get by, but were a valuable addition to the party. You'll want someone close to share your experiences with; it seems somehow rather hollow to enjoy the experience of a lifetime with some hitchhiker you've known for two weeks. As long as she's not the type who is terrified by a cockroach and empties the ashtray each time you use it, she will probably get along just fine.

At left is Canadian hitchhiker Boyd McBride; in the center our Touareg "blue man" passenger; to the right, John Ibbotson, a hitchhiker picked up in mid-Sahara.

HITCHHIKERS:

What about hitchhikers? After I was given a badly needed lesson in hospitality, I picked up everything from a Spanish deep-sea diver to a Touareg "blue man".

Moroccan Arabs had hustled, hassled, and had me so often that I had developed a deep distrust of all natives. I was cured one day when we became hopelessly mired in about two feet of loose sand, right in the middle of the road. After a while, some five natives drove up in an aging Land Rover pickup truck. With little or no discussion, they energetically dug us clear and pushed us out a total of four times, making about five yards progress each time. They wouldn't even let us help dig, taking away my shovel to do the work themselves. I had become so paranoid about theft that my sole interest throughout the entire performance was to be sure the shovel got put back into the van each time, so that it wouldn't conveniently disappear.

Finally, they towed us out with the truck, breaking a spring shackle in the process. Now, according to my prior experience, it was time for the heated argument about how much they would overcharge us. I was properly put down when, instead of demanding money, these helpful souls explained cheerfully that they would stay and repair their spring, but that we should go on ahead, as it would be dark soon. I felt only partially redeemed after a half hour lying on my back in the sand while I helped with their repairs. Thereafter, I was a little more benevolent toward the occasional desert dweller.

About that Touareg blue man: The blue men are a nomadic, pastoral tribe, who dress entirely in blue, from midnight-hued turban to toe-length, royal blue robe. As if to heighten the effect, they habitually chew a substance that dyes their lips, teeth, and hands—you guessed it—a deep blue.

While we were stopped along the track in northern Niger, one of these colorful gentlemen approached the camper, made gestures of friendship, and made known his desire to ride south with us. We declined in friendly fashion. Undaunted, he approached me, took my hand in his, and stood holding my hand and gazing at me warmly. There I stood, in the middle of the Sahara Desert, holding hands with a male primitive, to whom I could not communicate a single word, and who was swathed, literally from head to foot, in about twenty yards of blue fabric. I dared not reject his offer of friendship by removing my hand, at least until a decent interval had passed; I just stood there feeling silly. Periodically, my new found friend would point at himself, at me, at the camper, and then to the road south. I would shake my head.

Eventually, I managed to escape to the inside of the camper. Within moments, my Touareg appeared at the open side door, and motioned that he wanted water. As I drew a glass for him, he sat down, as if very weary, on the floor just inside the door. Water in hand, he slyly insinuated himself into the vehicle, until, after several minutes, he had worked his way onto the rear seat. He sat there grinning hugely. No amount of coaxing could get him out.

Within minutes, I was laughing so hard that I happily took him along with us to Tegguiddan, half a day's drive off. He obviously enjoyed the trip immensely, and must have gained incalculable status upon arriving at the village in such grand fashion.

Desert dwellers often asked us for rides, sometimes in the opposite direction from that in which they were headed, just because the automobile was such a fantastic novelty to them—like a trip to Mars for you or me. I think they would gladly have walked back ten miles just to receive a ten-mile ride.

Much later, in Central Africa, hundreds of natives flagged us down just to bum a smoke. In sheer self defense, we stopped stopping.

You will probably encounter a surprising number of young people, mostly British and Canadian, hitchhiking throughout Africa. Almost to a man, those I met were companionable, trustworthy, penniless, and lazy. Picking them up will do you no harm, and may brighten your day.

THE ALL-IMPORTANT VEHICLE

While waiting for our clearance in Adrar, we met some truly colorful characters: an Englishman, an Irishman, and a girl, crossing the Sahara in a bright yellow, London taxicab. This heavily laden, unmodified vehicle had front engine, two-wheel drive, and about six inches of ground clearance.

Naturally enough, the Prefect was hesitant to let them pass. So they told the authorities that they were traveling south with a convoy of seasoned explorers by the Gao-Timbuktu route. They then set out alone, heading east to In Salah, in their woefully ill-equipped vehicle. To make matters even hairier, they left the main track to take a much rougher, little used shortcut. We took the conventional track to In Salah the following morning.

Despite repeated inquiries on our part, we never saw or heard from the London cab again. To this day, I suspect that the three of them died out there somewhere, their vehicle half buried in all that soft sand.*

At the other extreme, in Agadez, we encountered a young Englishman and his petite German wife; they were walking, with completely self-contained backpacks, from south to north across the desert. They had lived in Africa for a number of years, had carefully prepared for the trip, and knew what they were about. At the time, they were already a third of the way across. I see no reason why they should not have reached their destination safely.

---

* Shortly before this book went to press, I learned that the London cab made it after all. They were bogged down and stranded for several days before being rescued from a desolate stretch of desert—an experience you won't want to imitate.

FOUR-WHEEL DRIVE:

Is four-wheel drive really necessary? My backpacking friends might contend that not even a vehicle is essential; but don't forget that London taxi lost somewhere between Adrar and In Salah.

I made it in an unmodified VW camper. I got buried in sand to the extent that a four-wheel-drive vehicle had to pull me out a round dozen times. We pushed, dug, and jockeyed it out by hand on countless occasions. Ed Everts' four-wheel-drive Land Rover bogged down once during the entire trip, then walked out under its own power.

Take your pick.

MODIFICATIONS:

If you insist on getting along with two-wheel drive, some vehicle modifications will make the going easier.

Extra wide tires and wheels are a valuable addition. A competent machinist can split your wheels vertically and add two or more inches of width. When completed, be sure to see them spun on a lathe or wheel hub. If they are wobbly or uneven, start over. Approximate cost in the U.S.: $8 to $10 per wheel. Don't forget to include a couple of extra wheels for your spare tires.

Tires should be as wide as the wheels, or perhaps a little wider. You may have to widen or cut out your wheel wells to accommodate them; check before you start.

A limited-slip differential would be a big help. Do *not* lock the rear end by welding, though. You would be far more likely to break an axle on the fast, paved roads, or in really rough terrain.

A lower-geared differential will give you additional power to plough through all that sand and mud, at the cost of a slightly lower top speed. Too expensive? Try going from 15″ tires and wheels to 14″, or from 16″ to 15″. The effect is the same, except that your ground clearance will be reduced.

One enterprising motorist manufactured a set of hexagonal studs, several inches long, one end with a female thread, the other male. When the going got too rough for his VW van, he removed the lug nuts from his rear wheels, screwed on the studs in their place, slipped an extra backing plate onto the outboard, male ends of the studs, then bolted his spare tire and wheel onto the protruding threads, using the original lug nuts. Each of the ten lugs looked something like this:

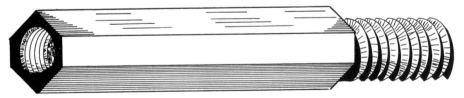

This end screws onto existing lug bolt.
It must be rounded to the same contour
as the lug nut.

Extra backing plate and spare tire and
wheel are held on this end by lug nut.

Result: Instant dual rear wheels, and increased traction and flotation.

High road clearance is essential. My 1970 camper bottomed way too many times for comfort. (The older models look a little higher.) Each time we hit bottom hard, my front stabilizer bar was bent down and back several inches. In retrospect, it seems that I spent half the trip underneath that van, bending the stabilizer bar back into plumb, using an old axle shaft for leverage. After awhile, the thing assumed the approximate dimensions of an oversized pretzel. While traveling through the Congo, we finally hit a huge rock and tore it off the car altogether. If you drive a VW van, you might remove the front stabilizer bar before setting out, or manufacture a pair of brackets to attach it rigidly to the front axle housing.

Switching to wheels and tires of a larger diameter would increase your clearance, but would also rob you of badly needed power.

Helper springs, heavy-duty shock absorbers, and stiffer suspension generally would be a considerable help. Sheet-steel armor plating, bolted or screwed in place to protect your steering arms, crankcase, and fuel tank, is another improvement; but leave holes for access to grease nipples, nuts and bolts, and mechanical parts. These additions must be tailored to the individual vehicle. They are not cheap, but are worth the added expense.

If you drive a VW or other rear-engine vehicle, your rear wheels will throw vast quantities of sand into the engine compartment, to be sucked directly into your carburetors. I cleaned about a pint of fine, red dust out of my air filter almost daily. Consider venting the intake of your air cleaner to the inside of the vehicle, by adding a length of heater hose.

PICK YOUR POWER:

Diesel engines are more reliable, need fewer parts, seldom require repairs, and run well for long periods under load. They have no points, plugs, or distributors, the source of most automotive breakdowns, and get almost twice the mileage of gasoline engines. In addition, diesel fuel costs far less than gas in most parts of the world.

Consequently, diesels have several advantages: greatly reduced fuel costs; less weight of fuel carried; less storage space pre-empted by fuel and parts; and less need to buy fuel where it is most expensive. Then again, diesel engines are expensive to buy initially, and are heavier than conventional power plants.

A word of caution: if you opt for the diesel; take along a set of extra injection nozzles, and learn how to clean and replace them before leaving. If you do have trouble, this is the most likely source.

Diesel mechanics may be harder to find when needed. Since desert towns are provisioned almost exclusively by diesel-powered lorries, however, this should not be too great a problem.

All things considered, I'd pick the diesel.

CAMPERS, THE ONLY WAY TO GO:

The ease and comfort of your own little house on wheels just can't be beat. We lazed about nightly in the VW, enjoying the clear, crisp desert air, while Captain Deb, Superboot, and crew pitched tents, built fires, and struggled with gear and equipment far into the night. On several occasions, I was invited to sleep in someone's home, but declined in favor of my own comfortable mobile home.

Certain little comforts go a long way toward making the desert or an East African rainy season livable: bed sheets, running water, butane heaters, built-in stoves, and window screens—above all else, window screens. In a camper, any reasonably quiet, city street is your lodging place. Restaurants and hotels become unnecessary. You avoid considerable expense. And you are with your gear at night to avert its theft.

The only real disadvantage is that the camper makes you too independent. You don't really have to get out and meet the native on his terms to get a meal or a place to sleep. But then, you can always force yourself.

MAKES AND MODELS:

The VW camper may be great to live in, but it does get stuck. Ground clearance is marginal. No four-wheel drive, low-range transmission, or diesel engine are available. Parts and service are spottily available and exorbitantly priced in Central Africa, plentiful but still expensive in the East and South. Gas mileage, dependability and toughness are excellent. The all-welded steel body does not develop rattles or shake apart; and the shoe-box shape doesn't waste an inch of living space. Initial cost is low; I paid about $3200 at the factory in Wiedenbruck, Germany. After returning to the U.S., I resold it privately for $2,900. An older van can be bought for peanuts.

A ZF limited-slip differential, designed for racing Porsches and Volkswagens, is available from Motion Minicar Corp., 594 Sunrise Highway, Baldwin, New York 11510, for $300. It can also be specially ordered from the Volkswagen factory. My local VW dealer quoted me $364 on pre-1968 models, and $503 for '68 and later. He could not guarantee time or delivery. Better try Motion Minicar first.

For further information, see your local VW dealer, or write: Customer Relations, Volkswagen of America, Englewood Cliffs, New Jersey 07632.

Despite a long and happy association with Jeeps in the U.S., I can't recommend them for Africa. For one thing, I was told repeatedly that they break a lot. Practically no parts or service exist, as is true for most American vehicles. They do not come with diesel; and even the Wagoneer is a shade snug to live in. Peace Corpsmen and other Americans in Africa can't get rid of them fast enough.

Ford Broncos and International Harvester Scouts are practically unheard of in Africa. Like Jeeps, they are reasonably sturdy, four-wheel drive vehicles, with gas power and small bodies. Parts and service will present a problem, although Ford has better coverage than any other American manufacturer.

Toyota Land Cruisers are becoming more and more popular in East Africa. They are dependable and sturdy, have four-wheel drive, and can be bought in a station-wagon-sized model that could be converted into a slightly cramped camper. Price in this country for the station wagon: about $4,800. No diesel. Parts and service do not exist outside East Africa; imagine having to order parts from Tokyo when you are stranded in Tamanrasset. Better pass this one up until it's had some seasoning.

The long-wheel-base Land Rover is the odds-on favorite. It is available as a camper fitted out by Dormobile, a British concern, at about $7,000 per copy. Write to: Dormobile Ltd., Folkestone, Kent, England, Attn: Mr. F. Kelly, Export Sales. Even without the camping equipment, it cost almost $5,000. The short-wheel-base four-cylinder petrol version, at $4,300, is the only model available in the U.S. The long wheel base diesel models cannot be imported, as they have not been certified by the U.S. Government. You would have to sell such a vehicle before returning.

The Land Rover features four-wheel drive and low-range transmission, rugged but uncomfortable suspension system, and rustproof aluminum body. It is exceptionally strong and reliable, and is almost big enough to live in. Most important, enough scrap parts can be found in almost any African junk heap to rebuild the entire thing from the ground up. Disadvantages: the aluminum body sucks dust into the passenger compartment like a giant vaccuum cleaner; the non-cab-over-engine design wastes all that good living space over the hood; and the gas tank holds a paltry twelve gallons. Outsized fuel tank is an optional extra.

For more information, write British Leyland Motors, 600 Willow Tree Road, Leonia, New Jersey 07605.

The long version of the Jeep Wagoneer, Toyota Land Cruiser, and Land Rover are all about the same size. None are quite long enough or high enough for comfortable living, although the Land Rover Dormobile camper makes it by dint of clever planning and an enormous pop-top.

An interesting evaluation of four-wheel-drive vehicles can be found in the September, 1972, issue of *Consumer Reports*. If available, copies may be ordered from Consumers Union, P.O. Box 1000, Orangeburg, New York 10962. If they are out of stock, try your local public library.

An American style, pickup-truck camper presents a bit of a quandary. The higher, bed-over-cab design provides adequate living space, but is a little topheavy for soft sand and deep mud. The low-profile type is within reasonable weight limitations; but nearly half its length is taken up by cab and hood, leaving minimal living room. Front engine, two-wheel drive, and poor gas mileage just about rule out most models.

Any four-wheel-drive pickup with low-range transmission, reasonably economical engine, and low-profile camper insert will do the job, if you can get by with less living area. They are manufactured by all of the big three, plus International, Jeep, Land Rover, and Datsun.

The mobile homes manufactured by Winnebago, Open Road, and other American manufacturers won't go ten feet off the pavement without bogging down. Better leave 'em at home.

For some strange reason, no one seems to manufacture the ideal vehicle: a diesel powered, four-wheel-drive, cab-over-engine, cigar-box-shaped van.

The best answer for many is a homemade camper built into a second hand van of some sort. Initial cost is low; it can be designed to fit the individual owner's needs; and it can be abandoned if necessary without bringing on bankruptcy proceedings. With luck, you might even find a four-wheel-drive lorry to convert. The British Government conducts surplus sales of just such vehicles in London from time to time. Notice of these sales is by advertisement in *Farmer and Stockbreeder,* and *Farmer's Weekly,* both published extensively throughout the United

Kingdom. Exceptional bargains occur for two reasons: such equipment is not of much use in England, except for pulling farm equipment; and all vehicles over a specified age must be sold, regardless of condition. Prices are in the $200 to $500 range. Models to look for are the Austin Champ, Humber Estate, and the Bedford R Model.

As far as African driving is concerned, right-hand as opposed to left-hand drive is pretty much of a tossup. You will drive on the right in North, Central, and West Africa, and on the left in the East and South.

WHERE TO BUY:

The cost of shipping a vehicle from a U.S. port to Africa, from Africa back to the U.S., or from the States to Europe is pegged by the Southern Atlantic Shipping Conference at about $800, depending on cubic volume. Round-trip shipping would run $1,600, which pretty well eliminates home-grown vehicles. The Northern Atlantic Conference charges by weight, which is far cheaper. Residents of Canada and the northern United States might inquire of their local shipping agent about shipping from a North Atlantic port, to obtain the lower rate.

A huge, bearded Canadian friend named John Gobbels avoided the shipping problem entirely. He scrounged a delapidated VW van from the U.S. Embassy in Rabat, Morocco, in exchange for "hauling that piece of junk out of here." The bus had been abandoned at the airport by some unknown wanderer; since it had U.S. plates, the authorities had turned it over to the Embassy. Lacking a title certificate or registration, John obtained an extremely official looking letter from the Ambassador, replete with ribbons and seals, stating that the vehicle had been given to him. After a $200 investment in parts and repairs, John was on his way. As a sort of added bonus, the prior owner had left inside the van a full kilo (2.2 pounds) of top grade Moroccan hashish.

Fortunately, a wide range of used vehicles is available in Germany, England, and France. New VW's or Land Rovers are bought most cheaply in their respective countries of origin, and can be ordered with U.S. specifications from your local stateside dealer for European delivery. Used VW vans are plentiful; Land Rovers less so; and Land Rover campers almost unobtainable.

Outfitting in Europe can be difficult, especially if you are a do-it-yourself advocate. The language barrier and the limited selection of tools you can take to Europe by air will hamper your efforts. Metric sizes add to the confusion. Possibly the best solution is to fly to London, where you speak the language, and buy your new or used vehicle through an automobile dealer or newspaper ad, just as you would at home. If your purchase leaves you with some converting to do, it wouldn't hurt to buddy up to a carpenter and a mechanic at the local pub. Then you will have access to some tools, or can at least get a decent rate for their services.

You could do well to buy from returning U.S. citizens, either by watching the want ads in the *Herald Tribune,* available in any European city, or by waiting at the shipping office at the docks in Bremen, Germany, where many an American VW owner goes to have his car shipped home at those low, North Atlantic rates. This approach has the added advantage of providing you with a vehicle meeting U.S.

Shades of *Beau Geste*.

specifications, should you wish to bring it back with you or sell it to another American.

Driving your rig from anywhere in Europe to Algeciras, Spain, and taking the ferry across to Ceuta or Tangier, in Morocco, is a relatively simple matter.

If you are headed from south to north, plenty of used VW vans and Land Rovers are to be had in East and South Africa; but prices are relatively high, and red tape may be a nuisance. In order to protect her own infant auto industry, South Africa has a prohibitive import duty on vehicles imported for permanent use or resale. This will price many imported cars out of your reach. Among others, Volkswagens and Fords are manufactured there and can be purchased sans tax. Most African nations have similar restrictions.

East Africa is loaded with used VW vans that have been in the service of the various safari and rental outfits. These vehicles will look good, but may have many a hard mile on them, put there by uncaring native drivers in a hurry. Check carefully before buying.

WHEN TO BUY:

In Europe, prices and choice of vehicle are at their best in September and October, just after the end of the European camping season. Few Europeans care to keep their campers all winter long—and don't forget all those Americans returning home after a summer of sightseeing. Fortunately, this dovetails nicely with the only time to push off across the desert—November to January.

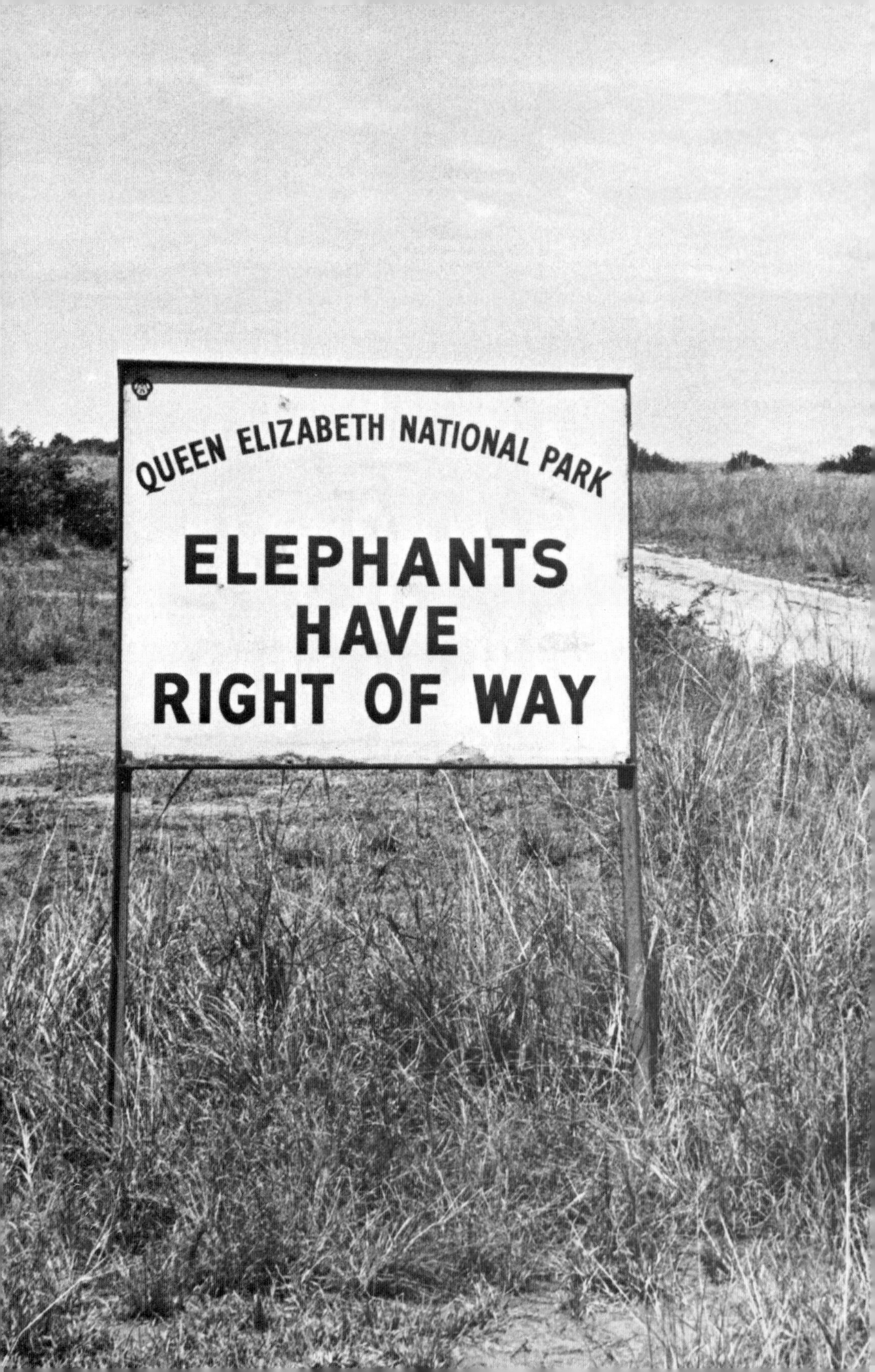
QUEEN ELIZABETH NATIONAL PARK
ELEPHANTS
HAVE
RIGHT OF WAY

AUTOMOTIVE

ODDMENTS

John Gobbels piloted his really beat-up VW van through part of our journey. During the particularly desolate, 437-mile stretch of desert between Tamanrasset, Algeria, and Assamaka, Niger, this venerable vehicle sheared a rocker-arm bolt clean off.

As it happened, John was travelling ahead of another vehicle in our party—an aging Land Rover—driven by three whimsical London barristers, Peter, Fran, and Tony. Fortunately, Peter was a capable amateur mechanic.

While John was busily engaged in stroking his beard and cursing his foul luck, Peter calmly removed the valve cover, extricated the broken bolt, glued the bolt together with Aerodyte aircraft cement*, and tempered the weld over a hastily built fire. When we parted company, several hundred miles later, it was still holding.

Be prepared.

TIRES AND WHEELS:
For extra traction, mount the widest wheels and tires practicable. You might even go to temporary dual rear wheels, as explained in the last chapter.

Use heavy-duty, lugged, mud or sand tires, if available. Snow tires with the studs removed should do the job. Military or truck tires are fine, but may be unmitigated hell to separate from the wheel with a pair of tire irons. Avoid tubeless tires. They are extremely difficult to break loose from the rim; and they'll need tubes anyway after they get their first rock cut.

*Available generally throughout the United Kingdom.

A word to the wise.

A wealth of makes is available. The heavy-duty Avons that can be purchased on a new Land Rover are fine. The Continental Swiss is an excellent lugged tire for Volkswagens. Michelins and Sears-Michelins resist cut sidewalls with steel-cord construction; they wear like spring steel.

You will have to balance your wheel and tire size between two factors: using a larger diameter to increase ground clearance, against using a smaller size to increase power. This is best resolved on an individual basis.

If you can find room, carry eight tires and six wheels for the full transcontinental trip, so you won't be caught short. In any event, carry at least two mounted, ready-for-use spares; and start out with new tires. Don't forget a couple of extra tubes.

The choice of tire brands and sizes is extremely limited in most North and Central African countries. In Morocco, only Moroccan-made General tires are sold; in Algeria, only Michelin. And you may find that, although you started out with a standard size in Europe or the States, it's considered an oddball in the French-speaking countries if it doesn't fit a Renault or Peugeot.

I personally went through three complete sets of standard highway tires. Since I carried only one spare, I had many an anxious moment running spareless on bald rubber.

In the Republic of Central Africa and the Congo, filling stations are scarce, and often offer no tire-repair services. Likely as not, a gas point shown on the map will turn out to be a corrugated iron shed. You pull up, take a piece of hose and a five-gallon can inside, stick the hose into a drum of petrol, suck gas to get the siphon started, fill your can, and go outside to pour it into your tank. Repeat until tank and all cans are filled. Obviously, you'd better be prepared to fix your own punctures.

After each blowout, we had to jack up the car, remove the wheel and tire, put on the spare, and go find a mission or filling station to borrow a foot pump. We would then jack up the car a second time with the jack resting on the side of the blown-out tire to break the bead, and jack it up a third time to break loose the bead on the other side. Next, we had to pry the tire halfway off the wheel with two tire irons, remove the tube, locate the leak, patch the tube, and patch the inside of the tire if broken or cut. It was still necessary to replace the tube, pry the tire back onto the rim, pump it up by foot, and remount the wheel and tire.

During a four-day period in the Republic of Central Africa, I went through the above procedure exactly 14—that's right, 14—times.

Oddly enough, after we crossed into the Congo, riding on the same bald tires, on even rougher roads, we had no more flats. We came to the conclusion that this was because most of our punctures had been caused by scrap metal, nails, bits of wire, and other metal objects. The Congo, in contrast, has grown so poor that it literally does not have any scrap metal or nails to lie about.

Some tire-changing tips: Recalcitrant beads can be broken loose from the rim by jacking up the vehicle with the base of the jack resting on the side of the tire, as close as possible to the edge of the rim; when you have one side loose, flip the tire over and repeat for the other side. Always check the inside of the tire for cuts and breaks, which will flex when the tire is in use and pinch another hole in the tube; if a break can be seen or felt, put a patch over it. A little soapy water or dishwashing detergent on the tire bead will make levering the tire on and off the rim far easier. Place a piece of plywood or sheet steel under the jack base when working in sand or mud; it is most discouraging to jack your jack down into the sand, while your car moves not an inch.

Never, ever jack up your car without first blocking a wheel. Failure to do so will almost invariably result in lost time, bent jacks, and broken arms. None of the three are easily replaceable.

Before you start out, practice! Find out whether your tire irons are adequate, the pump works, your patches hold, and your tires are not too stiff to get on and off by hand. And make sure your lug wrench is not one of those cheap, soft-iron jobs that twist apart in your hands as soon as you lean on them.

Do not rely on your manufacturer's bumper jack. Bring it, but include a good, hydraulic jack also. You'll need it, especially after the bumper jack gets bent. The tall, jeep jacks popular for woods use in the U.S. should do the job, if you can manage to take one over with you on the airplane.

A word about African service stations. Tires are loosened from the rim by pounding the small end of an axle shaft, held vertically, on them—hard on the tire, and even harder on the rim when someone's aim is off a little. Usual cost of repair; under $1.00 per patch; but beware: one blowout might require three or four patches at $1.00 each.

Spare tire brackets, to mount your spares outside the car, are invaluable, as spares take up an inordinate amount of space. Ensure that they are firmly bolted through good-sized, steel butt plates, so they won't tear loose.

THE LUGGAGE RACK;

Roof racks for gas cans, luggage, tools, and equipment are also invaluable. You will undoubtedly be short of storage space and will appreciate the added room. Such a rack can make the difference between having and not having enough petrol, water, and tires to survive.

Be sure your rack is securely attached, as it will be carrying a lot of weight through a lot of bouncing around. It should be fastened by one of three methods: welded in several places; securely bolted with heavy bolts through steel butt plates or fender washers, to spread out the strain; or firmly attached to the rain gutter.

The factory rack on the VW camper is secured along the rear edge with two sheet-metal screws. Mine came half off the car several times before we finally got it firmly bolted down, and repaired the resulting roof leaks.

Don't forget shock-cord, hold-down straps to keep the contents in the rack. The type with several straps joined together in the center and faintly resembling an octopus are especially versatile. Bring extras; you'll find many other uses for them. Commonly called Bungee cords, they can be bought anywhere in Europe, and in many parts of Africa. An added convenience, but optional, is a waterproof, canvas cover, that straps snugly down over the contents of the rack. They are for sale at the VW factory in Wiedenbruck, to fit VW campers, for about $20.

GAS CANS:

You will undoubtedly need spare petrol cans. If you follow the Hoggar track (as we did), you will travel 557 miles without a gas point; on the Gao-Timbuktu route, even farther. Even on short trips, you should carry at least one five-gallon can for emergencies.

Compute your gas consumption through sand at about 150% of normal. If, for instance, you normally get 20 miles per gallon, and are following the Hoggar track, your true consumption, instead of one gallon every 20 miles, will be 1½ gallons per 20 miles, or 7½ gallons per 100 miles. Figuring 600 miles to allow for meandering and getting lost, you will actually burn up 45 gallons. Adding another five gallons for emergency use (always add five gallons for emergency use) results in a recommended capacity of 50 gallons. We carried 50 gallons, and arrived in Agadez with an empty gas tank and one full five-gallon can. Always overfigure; carrying a little extra won't hurt.

Gasoline, by the way, is never "gas," but "essence" (rhymes with "wants") in the French-speaking countries, and "petrol" in English-speaking areas. It is sold in liters rather than gallons. A liter is about 34 ounces, slightly more than a quart. You might also encounter the British imperial gallon, which is approximately 156 ounces to our 128, or about 22% larger. Petrol can be extremely expensive—About $1.00 per gallon in Tamanrasset and Agadez.

Gas cans are easily found anywhere in Europe, and in most civilized areas of Africa. Average price for the five-gallon or 20-liter size: $3 to $5. It pays to buy from travelers headed the other way, who are through the desert, as they no longer need their gas cans, sand ladders, etc., and don't want to carry unnecessary gear. You can even pick up some equipment free at one or two dumps along the track; but don't depend on it. Be sure to purchase a gas-can spout or funnel with a fine mesh strainer in it, and use it always. You only need to fill your tank with dirty or watered petrol once to bring the entire convoy to a screeching halt.

If heading from north to south, try to buy your gas cans before leaving Europe, as you can fill them at Ceuta, a Spanish free port, for about .20 per gallon.

You will also need water cans. We carried 12½ gallons for three people, and always had a comfortable margin. Water is far more plentiful than gas. Be sure to mark your water cans in some unmistakable way, so that you won't accidentally pour them into your gas tank, or fill them with petrol by mistake. Such an error could be truly disastrous. Don't buy collapsible, plastic water containers; you will use up all your tire patches, as did Ed Everts, repairing the cracks that develop.

Gas-can racks, such as those seen on Jeeps and Land Rovers, will give you added storage space. The Land Rover type, designed to rest on a bumper, are best. If they are merely bolted to the side of the vehicle, be sure a large, steel butt plate is used, to prevent vibration and bouncing from tearing it loose from the body.

SAND LADDERS:

Sand ladders are so named because the Land Rover factory type are actually steel ladders. In fact, they are made from any long, flat, metal objects that can be laid out in front of each tire to keep it from digging further into the sand. Most popular are military, aircraft-landing-strip sections, and lengths of heavy-duty wire fencing. Get the landing-strip sections if you can find them. The wire fencing will begin to curl after being used a few times; simply turn them over after each use.

Procedure for use is as follows: After you get stuck, dig out all four wheels and a space under your engine, transmission, and rear axle. Then dig two trenches in front of your tires, gradually sloping up to ground level. Add a third trench in the center if your differential or crankcase will be dragging. Lay sand ladders in front of all four tires, wedging them as far under the tires as possible. It helps to let your tires down to about eight or ten pounds pressure (but bear in mind that sooner or later you'll just have to pump them all back up again). All passengers push, while the driver gives it the gun in the lowest gear. Avoid excessive wheel spin, but give it plenty of power. With luck, you may make as many as five or ten yards before starting over again. An occasional swearword is not inappropriate. Repeat until you hit solid ground.

Sand ladders are not for sale generally. You will have to find them in a dump or scrounge them from travelers bound in the other direction. However you do it, get at least two, preferably four.

Try to mount them outside the vehicle someplace where you can get at them easily. You may need them often, and you won't want to mess up the inside of the car with sand and scratch up the paint taking them in and out. Be sure to tie them down tightly—here's where your extra hold-downs come in handy.

COMPASSES:

In Spain, I had insisted upon buying a compensatable compass to replace my non-adjustable one, over the vociferous objections of my two passengers (we were sharing the $4.50 expense). Later, on a due north-south Moroccan road, we compensated it to point true North. The old compass turned out to be as much as 40° off.

Much later still, we reached a vast, sand plain near the Niger border. To avoid the washboarded sand, vehicles there leave the road ruts and take off cross-country, leaving literally scores of sets of tracks. We followed what looked like the majority of tracks, and tried to stay with the heaviest concentration each time they forked. After crossing some quite rocky ground, we found ourselves following a single pair of tracks that disappeared into a huge, soft-sand erg (a sort of flat dune).

My companions insisted that we follow those tracks. Even level-headed John Ibbotson stubbornly voted to go on. "He made it," he summed up simply, pointing at the two tracks we had been following.

"How do you know he made it?" I demanded heatedly. "How do you know we won't find his skeleton out there somewhere, bleaching in the sun? Besides, he might have been in a Land Rover. We have two-wheel drive, and no one behind us to pull us out." (Ed's Land Rover was now two days behind, delayed initially by John Gobbels' rocker arm bolt, and running more slowly anyway with four-wheel drive.) "From the looks of things," I added, "a car comes by here about once a year. We could be stuck out there forever."

Eventually, we retraced our own tracks, until we lost them on the rocky ground, and were really and truly lost. We now had no tracks to follow, and had no idea whether we were north, south, east, or west of the main road. I climbed atop the van and studied the horizon in all directions with an eight-power, telescopic camera lens; the desert was a featureless expanse in every direction. John walked around the camper in a circle several hundred yards across, looking for tracks. Nothing. The map revealed only what we already knew: that the road ran from Northeast to Southwest. But in which direction did it lie? We were reasonably sure to be within about five miles of it, but which way?

After some long and careful thought, and no little heated discussion, we determined to drive across country due north for fifteen miles, then turn right and proceed due east until we hit the track. That way, no matter which side of the road we were on, if it was within eight or ten miles in any direction, we must hit it eventually. If this doesn't make sense to you when expressed in words, the accompanying diagram demonstrates that it works.

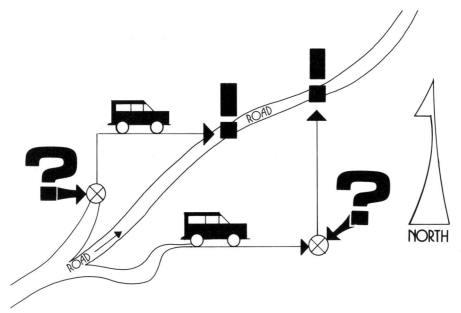

And work it did. Within about five miles, we found some multiple tracks headed northeast, and turned to follow them; they soon led us back to safety. Moral: buy a good automotive or marine compass with compensating magnets, mount it in plain view of the driver, and compensate it yourself. And when in doubt, triangulate.

About compass variation: I was unable to determine the correct variation for North Africa. Even the Michelin maps, so complete in every other detail, fail to mention this important factor. I simply compensated the compass to geographic north, and ignored the variation. This works out fine, and is much simpler to work with, so long as you are not concerned with pin-point accuracy. The variation changes considerably as you travel thousands of miles from north to south. Better check your compass against a true north-south or east-west road periodically.

LIGHTS:

Another handy gadget is a hand-held spotlight, with a long wire hooked up to your cigarette lighter or fuseblock. Connecting your on-off switch to a relay will prevent the switch from burning up. Such a rig is easily made from a scrap foglight or driving light. A 12-volt, aircraft-landing-light sealbeam will fit a standard foglight, and provides lots of illumination. Wire it like this:

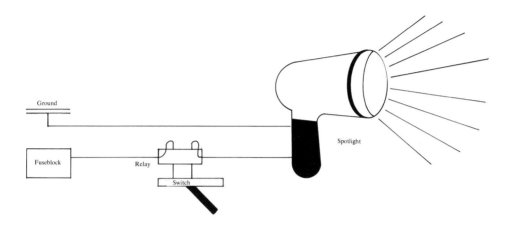

You should also carry at least one flashlight. Get the standard, cylindrical type, which takes D sized batteries, as replacements are available in nearly every African village. Take a pair of spare bulbs along, though. The larger, rectangular dry cells popular in the States cannot be found readily in Africa. Don't buy a cheapie—it will work about half the time.

It wouldn't hurt to carry an extra automobile battery. If you do, be sure to wire it into your electrical system, so that it will be charged by the generator. An uncharged battery is of little use. A pair of jumper cables is a desirable alternative.

TOOLS:

Do not, under any circumstances, buy cheap tools. You will pay for them many times over in blood, sweat, and frustration. There are no hardware stores to sell you replacements in Tegguiddan. Get the best you can afford.

It is important to try all tools on your vehicle before leaving. An American socket set that won't fit your metric nuts and bolts is next to worthless.

For a list of tools that will cover most normal maintenance and emergencies, see Appendix VI. Leave out any you consider superfluous, but only if you have something else that will do the job.

SPARES:

Spare parts should also be tested and fitted before embarking. There is little point wasting space on parts that don't fit—and you could get stranded. A basic list is in Appendix VI.

CAMPING SCAM

As we jounced along the track between Assamaka and Tegguiddan, almost 90 miles from the nearest town, we spotted a distant figure moving slowly toward us along the trail. After a time, we reached him and stopped to talk.

Verbal communication turned out to be impossible, for lack of a common language. With smiles, nods, and signs, we fed our guest water and food, and determined only that he was walking to some distant point in the direction from which we had come.

Our bronze-skinned friend was dressed in the inevitable, head-to-foot robe of the desert nomad. He carried about his neck and beneath his robe a small skin of water, and an even tinier bag containing some bits of food and perhaps some few, small possessions.

Ultimately, we left him to trudge on alone through that scorched wasteland, and followed his footprints South along the road. We could not help wondering aloud about our friend's starting point and destination, his manner of survival, and his purpose of travel. After several miles, the footprints suddenly turned and angled off into empty desert, whence he had come.

That man was carrying the minimum of camping equipment.

Almost as austere were John Ibbotson and Jaime, whom we picked up near Arak. John was a short, round-faced Briton, with clipped speech, who looked and sounded for all the world like Richard Burton. Jaime was a high-born Spaniard from Barcelona (in his classical, Castilian accent, "Barfthelona"), turned deep-sea diver and wanderer. John carried a small shoulder bag and a duffel bag, most of whose contents consisted of discarded clothing to be traded to the natives. Jaime toted a single, overnight-type satchel.

Domestic tranquility.

When night came, John would happily scoop out a grave-like indentation in the sand, unroll his sleeping bag, and climb in, fully dressed, for a night's sound slumber. Jaime would curl up under the camper or near the fire with nothing but his one blanket and whatever additional coverings he could scrounge. Neither carried cooking equipment, tents, or other such folderol.

Of course, it's not really necessary to be quite that uncomfortable.

TENTS AND TENTING:

My strongest recommendation is to possess a vehicle suitable for sleeping. This arrangement protects you from insects, rain, cold, prowlers, animals, and what have you, with a minimum of trouble and bother. And it can be used in cities.

Failing this, you will want a tent. Size will, of course, depend upon the number of people to be accomodated. Above all else, keep it small and simple. You will be on the move most of the time, and will have to erect it once a day and stow it once a day. The heavier and bulkier your tent, the more you will learn to hate it. Just be sure it's big enough to cover its occupants, together with all their gear and luggage.

No tent will be livable without a built-in, watertight floor and screened openings for ventilation. An added convenience, but not really essential, is a fly sheet (double roof) for insulation against the heat and improved leakage resistance. A pop-up frame will greatly reduce the hassle of erecting, especially in sandy areas, where tent pegs do not hold well. Unfortunately, it's an expensive luxury. Nylon is the material of choice; it is far more lightweight, compact, and waterproof than canvas.

Take lots of long, strong tent pegs. You'll lose them, break them, and watch them pull loose in the sand time after time. Pegs with a broad, paddle-like profile will provide added holding power. The new, plastic pegs won't bend like metal or splinter like wood.

Tent bargains require some looking. After pricing two-man, nylon, mountain tents at $35 and up, I recently bought one manufactured by Camel, 329 S. Central St., Knoxville, Tennessee 37902, at a local Gold Triangle store, for just under $15. It required some reinforcing at points of strain; but at that price, I can't complain.

SLEEPING BAGS:

A warm sleeping bag is a must. Nights are quite chilly in the desert and throughout most of Africa. The entire continent, except for the coastal regions, consists of a mile-high plateau; so cool nights can be expected everywhere, despite the season. The mercury seldom drops below freezing, however.

A goose down bag is recommended as providing the most warmth per pound of weight and per cubic foot of storage space. Good ones can be had without mortgaging the family homestead from: Black's of Greenock, in London, for about $30; or Arthur Ellis and Co., Private Bag, Dunedin, New Zealand, for about $35. They can be had in the U.S. at higher prices. Try: L. L. Bean, Inc., Freeport, Maine 04032; Gander Mountain, Inc., P.O. Box 248, Wilmot, Vermont 53192; or Parker Distributors, 40 Industrial Place, New Rochelle, New York 10805. Next best are duck down bags, available from Arthur Ellis for under $20. You can get by nicely with a good polyester bag, if you can't stand the expense.

Try to find a bag with a zipper that opens all the way down one side and across the bottom, so you won't drown in your own perspiration on warm nights. Such a bag can be opened up for use as a quilt, or zipped together with a matching bag to hold two good friends.

A sleeping bag liner is a must. You will retire on some nights covered with a fine dust the color of red ocher, and on other nights just after your first bath in a week. You'll welcome a method of keeping your bag clean. A liner is easily made by sewing an old bed sheet in the shape of the bag, but a trifle smaller. Add buttons or snaps to attach liner to bag at the head and foot ends, so that you won't wake up at 3:00 A.M. wrapped in swaddling clothes.

If you travel by camper, you might substitute a warm comforter or heavy blankets, as you'll be sleeping comfortably in a real bed. In that case, make a custom fitted, bottom sheet to fit your mattress; it will never stay in place otherwise. If you ever part from the camper, you'll have a definite luggage problem with this rig.

HEATERS, STOVES, AND LANTERNS:

Heaters are not really essential, but they sure are nice to have along. You can build a fire for warmth, unless you are in a city, it is raining, or there is nothing to burn. Stoves and lanterns can double as heaters in an emergency. A gasoline heater that does a magnificent job without overtaxing the battery can be had as optional equipment with the VW camper. If you outfit in the U.S., try a South Wind gasoline heater; it will produce enough heat to drive you out of the car within five minutes after you turn it on.

As there is no wood throughout most of the Sahara, it is common practice to pick up an old, discarded, truck tire along the road each day; at night, a liter or so of petrol is poured over the tire to create a crackling bonfire. Of course, it's not exactly fragrant, and you have to stay upwind of it; but it burns a long time, throws lots of heat, and it is available. If you're on an ecology kick, don't get too upset at this. The Sahara desert is one of the few places left on earth where a cloud of black, oily smoke will bother neither man nor beast (that is, if the wind doesn't shift after you've lit it).

A two-burner stove is highly recommended, preferably installed semi-permanently in your camper. Cooking over an open fire may sound romantic, but it has its disadvantages. The heat is hard to control (you'll burn a lot of stews); it is messy (soot on the bottoms of your pots, burned food on the insides); it is sometimes unavailable (in cities or during rainstorms); and imagine having to pick up and carry two tires a day—one for dinner, and another for coffee in the morning. A single-burner stove is a real source of annoyance when you want to fix coffee and oatmeal, or soup and stew, at the same time.

A camper adequately outfitted with interior lights makes a lantern unnecessary. We used the inside lights in the VW almost nightly and did quite a bit of reading and writing, with no adverse effect on the battery. For camping out, you might rig up a simple, 12-volt light that can be clamped onto a handy tree limb or tent pole. A discarded taillight with the lens removed is adequate. Wiring is simplicity itself: just attach two wires ending in alligator clips to the battery's positive and negative posts.

Double-mantle lanterns provide substantially more light than the single-mantle version, at a slight increase in cost. Be sure to take several spare mantles. Before you start, arrange a method of packing your lantern during the day (perhaps in the carton it came in), so that the mantles and globe won't be broken by all that bouncing around.

Your heater, stove, and lantern should all use the same fuel. It is ridiculous to carry three different kinds of hard-to-locate fuel, when one will do.

Most practical is the Gaz line of butane equipment widely sold in Europe. Butane accessories burn clean, seldom need refueling, offer no messy and hazardous refilling problems, do not require pumping or cleaning, and have no generators or other troublesome parts to replace. They function as simply as the gas stove in your home. But beware: leakage can be extremely dangerous. Fortunately, butane has an easily detectable odor.

Butane is inexpensive, can be purchased anywhere in Europe, and is available in most of Africa's larger cities. Two three-liter bottles should be ample for the entire trip. When you purchase your equipment, you buy the filled bottles outright, then swap the empties for full ones at any Gaz dealer, for a charge of perhaps $2 per bottle. If no dealer can be found, or he does not have the big bottles, seek out the nearest butane plant and cut out the middleman—it's cheaper that way, anyhow.

Do not buy the Gaz equipment that utilizes the small, disposable cartouche, which lasts a much shorter time and is far more expensive per kilogram. It is ideal for backpackers or others with severely limited space, though.

Gaz equipment is sold at widely varying prices. Some approximate (very approximate) prices are: two-burner stove, $15; space heater, $9; lantern, $8; full three-kilogram bottle, $8; three-kilogram refill, $1.50.

Coleman or other white-gas burners are not recommended. For openers, no one in Europe or Africa ever heard of white gas, not to mention spare generators or other parts. If you burn ordinary petrol, you will be dismantling and cleaning the generator with great regularity, and will ultimately ruin it by deforming its tiny aperture.

I carried a Coleman stove (purchased new at an Army P.X. in Germany for $22) and an outsized kerosene heater all over Europe, until they both ceased functioning one bitter night in a Swiss mountain pass during a snowstorm. I gave up in disgust and gave them both to a friend in Torremolinos. Their Gaz replacements never failed to function perfectly.

If you must use Coleman-type equipment, you can burn benzine, or cleaning fluid, in it. However, it is expensive and hard to locate, and emits extremely noxious fumes when started up and extinguished. It is available in some European pharmacies, under the name, "benzine", "waschen bensin", or "rensit bensin".

If you can befriend an American soldier and get inside a P.X., you might find Coleman fuel. Unfortunately, this is an expensive solution; it takes a huge number of one-pint cans to last out a six-month trip. (I never saw the one-gallon size overseas.)

There are other types of equipment available: a German lantern that looks and functions just like a Coleman, but burns kerosene; British Primus stoves, that will burn almost anything; and the small-sized Aladdin heaters from England, which also burn kerosene.

If you outfit with butane appliances in the U.S., you should have a metric-to-American adapter, to get your tanks filled.

DON'T BE BUGGED:

While there are no insects in the uninhabited Sahara, they can be painfully present when human habitations are encountered. The flies in Tamanrasset, 430 miles from the next town, are endemic. In Central and East Africa, insects abound. In some parts of the Congo and Tanganyika, tsetse flies are a real hazard.

A screened camper or tent is your best protection. Mosquito netting can be purchased South of the desert; but you may need it before you find it for sale. Take with you at least enough to cover yourself while asleep.

Off and Raid are highly endorsed, the former as a repellent, the latter as a space spray. Both products were effective against all African insects encountered. Two large, spray cans of each lasted the entire trip.

A KITCHEN CHECKLIST:

Rule One: keep it simple. The more paraphernalia you carry, the more there is to store, clean, and handle. If you should run short, pots and pans, plates and cups are easily obtainable everywhere.

The items listed in Appendix VI should suffice for two people.

If you happen to be a dedicated coffeehound, you might prefer coffee strained through filter paper. Almost anywhere in Europe, you can purchase a small pottery or plastic filter-paper holder that sits atop a coffee cup, and packages of small, individual filter papers. Buy one holder, and one paper for each day of the trip, per person. Then you need only boil water each morning, and pour it right through the filter paper into your cup. It makes better coffee; there is no need to wash the pot; and your British friends can join you for a cup of tea or cocoa without heating a separate pot of water.

Teflon cookware is easiest to clean, a considerable advantage when camping. Cast iron heats more evenly, and in sandy country is quickly scoured out with a handful of sand. Try to find a set that nests together for more compact storage.

Get large, clay coffee cups. Metal cups transmit enough heat to burn your lips and hands; plastic ones often have an objectionable taste. Oversized mugs can double as soup bowls, drinking glasses, etc.

Don't waste your money and time on cheap knives. Buy a top-grade breadknife or butcher knife. (You'll eat lots of unsliced bread.) It is best kept in a sheath of some sort to keep it sharp. Serrated table knives or steak knives make mealtimes easier.

Salt and pepper shakers should have flip-top lids, to keep out dust and moisture.

In Central Africa, you'll need several one-liter bottles to contain your purified drinking water. Accumulate these in Europe or Morocco as you go along. Old beer or wine bottles are ideal. (Until recently, almost all beer was sold in one-liter bottles; an unfortunate move is afoot to reduce this man-sized portion to a mere 65 centiliters.)

INVALUABLE MISCELLANY:

Bring lots of Baggies. Everything in the desert, from day-old bread to photographic lenses, quickly acquire a coat of fine, tawny powder. A good quantity of the largest sized plastic bags will prove invaluable. You'll want to keep all your perishables and valuables in them. Once you leave Europe, they are unobtainable.

The most important item you'll carry is lots of soft, American-style toilet paper. There simply is none throughout the desert and most of Central Africa. What is available feels as if some of the splinters weren't removed. European paper is almost as bad, although some English brands will do. Best bring some with you from the States.

You'll need a plastic bucket or dishpan for doing your laundry. Most convenient is a standard plastic bucket, with sturdy wire handle and snug-fitting, water-tight lid. With this rig, you can throw your sox and underwear inside with some soapy water in the morning, hang the bucket somewhere where it will bounce around as you drive, empty and refill with rinse water once or twice during the day, and have clean clothing by afternoon. Total labor invested: almost zero.

Such a bucket will also come in handy for filling your water tank, impromptu showers, etc.

Highly recommended is Woolite. It will lather in almost any water on earth, removes the stubbornest dirt, and can be used for good wool sweaters and delicate clothing. Conventional detergents can be bought anywhere.

THAT FAVORITE HANDGUN:

Before entering the Congo, we were advised to stay a night at the mission school in Boomba, with M'sieu' David. A few hours motoring along a narrow, jungle path, lush foliage within touching distance on either side, brought us to Boomba—a typical, Congolese village, consisting of a handful of disintegrating, brick buildings left behind by the Belgians, and the inevitable, circular native huts.

Most of the emerging African nations have kept a few Europeans around, to guide them through the nuances of civilization as they learn to run a modern government. Not so in the sprawling, tropical nation known as the Democratic Republic of the Congo, recently renamed "Zaire" in a demonstration of anti-Europeanism. It has expelled nearly all Caucasians in a violent reaction against the Belgian occupation. As a result, the jungle is once again overgrowing everything, maintenance is nil (broken windows are simply covered over with boards or just left broken), roads are all but impassable, and the people live largely in the old, primitive manner. There are spectacular natural resources in the Congo, but no practical way to get them out. Air freight of ore or timber would be prohibitively expensive; she has no coastline for shipping; and the Congo River cannot be used, because it reaches the sea through her sister state, Republic of Congo, with whom she is in a state of incipient

The baobab thrives throughout most of southern Africa. Native legend has it that God punished the baobab tree by making it grow upside down, roots in the air.

belligerency. Creeping civilization is blotting out the natural world at such a rate that perhaps it is just as well that a sizable hunk of Africa will refrain, at least for a few years, from turning into a vast parking lot.

M'sieu' David (accent on the second syllable) turned out to be David Trokeloshvili, a lanky, bearded, Russo-American, who resembles a sort of skinny Shel Silverstein. David, an accomplished linguist, speaks eleven languages and collects genuine, native folk art in the form of ceremonial masks and statues.

We rolled up in convoy, seven complete strangers, and were welcomed warmly, given the unrestricted use of the premises, and offered anything we wanted from the skimpily stocked pantry. Living alone at a rural mission school, 405 of the hardest miles ever from what could even begin to qualify as a city, this gentle soul's hospitality had become legend throughout the area.

We stayed three days, were feasted and feted insofar as local resources allowed, and enjoyed ourselves thoroughly. On our last night, two Germans in an International truck drove up—boosting the total guest roster to nine—and were welcomed in the same open-handed fashion.

We received word from one of David's missionary friends that he had been asked by the government to relay a telegram instructing the nearby border officials to close the border and turn back all tourists. The missionary offered to delay the message until we could make good our escape to the south. It was, and is, virtually impossible to reach East Africa without traversing the Congo. If we could just get far enough south and east before getting caught, we would be thrown out to the east, where we were headed anyway, instead of to the north, which would leave us stranded. Thus began a driving marathon lasting several days; fortunately, it was successful.

We heard later that the cause of the border-closing incident was the unthinking act of a single tourist, at some other border post, attempting to bring an undeclared gun into the country.

Firearms of any kind, type, or description are absolutely and unconditionally verboten. African governments, often insecurely seated in power and subject to sudden coups and revolts, are extremely paranoid about potential revolutionaries or mercenaries. They will blow their minds at the mere sight or mention of a gun.

It is possible, of course, to bring a firearm into some countries for hunting purposes. In this case, a detailed application must be filed well in advance, permission obtained, and perhaps a bond posted. The red tape is considerable. If you are flying to Kenya for a hunting trip, then flying home, this is the recommended procedure. If you are wandering through twenty or so countries without a timetable, forget it. (Please don't go to Kenya, or anywhere else, for a hunting trip, by the way. Caught between encroaching civilization and the depredations of native poachers and ivory- and skin-traders, Africa's once-great animal population is engaged in a desperate struggle for life, and may be losing. 25 years from now, when no leopards or rhinos remain on earth, you won't want to have to think back to the time when you helped destroy them. You can be just as big a he-man, and have just as much fun, as I did, stalking your big game with a telephoto lens.)

The penalty for possession of an undeclared firearm ranges from immediate expulsion from the country to several years in the local penitentiary. I spoke at some length with an American girl in Bangui, R.C.A., who spent a few months in a Moroccan jail on drug charges. It is an experience you will want to miss. Even the remote possibility of an African jail sentence is sufficient cause to forbear from smuggling in your favorite handgun "just for self-protection".

You won't really need much protection, anyway. Most of the large animals are now confined to game parks, and won't bother you if you don't bother them. For protection against my fellow man, I kept a three-foot machete within easy reach, and only once came anywhere close to needing it.

Leave it at home, Bwana!

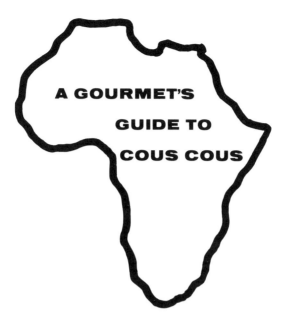

A GOURMET'S GUIDE TO COUS COUS

It had been my habit, in Paris, to frequent the Algerian area in the Latin Quarter. I quickly became hopelessly addicted to a meal of farina covered with a meat stew, called cous cous, the national dish of Algeria.

I had spent so much time talking up this fine comestible that my caravan comrades finally called my bluff. We sought out a native restaurant in Tamanrasset and ordered cous cous. The waiter was very sorry, but cous cous must be ordered a day in advance. (They may have needed time to slaughter a goat.) But we could have the ragout, which was "tres bon, M'sieu', tres bon."

And so it was that we ordered seven servings of stew, consisting of canned peas, gravy, and some unidentifiable and unappetizing pieces of meat. We ate amid boisterous speculation as to the contents of the stew. The meat was quite chewy and tasteless, and was covered with tiny bumps, much like pimples. Ah, well, we would find out when the waiter returned.

We were awaiting dessert when we finally pressed the waiter into answering our question. We had just eaten, it seems, a ragout of camel stomach.

Incredibly, we returned the next night for cous cous, which did not begin to compare with that served in the Quartier Latin. Neither meal did me the slightest harm.

At Zinder, at the very southern edge of the desert, we ate a meal that did do me some harm. We tried out another native restaurant, where we were served a delicious but overspiced meal of noodles and "biftec" in hot sauce. In a frenzy of masochism, I devoured mine and three other unfinished platefuls.

I awoke next morning with an explosion in my gut. We were parked in front of Zinder's sole hotel, in a long parking area which also fronted on the town's chief bar and only movie theater.

(A Central African movie is a sight to behold. The twin bill in Zinder consisted of a pair of real turkeys, *John Paul Jones* and *Vengeance of Spartacus*. Not in the least put off by the lack of quality, the audience roared, shouted, laughed uproariously, and booed the villain. The soundtrack was often inaudible. How wonderful it must be to be so easily and intensely entertained.)

I was camped in the town's center of activity. Several small stands selling miscellaneous trivia were erected there each evening. I remained in the lot into the night to be within easy striking distance of the hotel's European-style toilet facilities, for which I anticipated an urgent need.

I dozed in the camper, and awoke in darkness, semi-delirious and seized by a compelling urge to seek out that toilet. I got out of the camper and began to lock it. My next sensation was that of waking up all over again, lying in the dirt of the parking lot. I had passed out and lain there for who knows how long.

I managed to regain my feet, lock the van, and lurch toward the hotel. Again, I woke up in the dirt, this time in the center of the lot, flat on my backside. The people of the town were all about me, walking past, going about their business, and ignoring that strange white man lying there unconscious. When I got to my feet a second time, it was too late for the toilet; what I needed now was a shower. Two days later, without treatment and for no apparent reason, I was as sound as ever.

What struck me about the incident was that, of all the people in that lot, no one came to my aid, called a gendarme, or notified the hotel manager. On the other hand, no one stole my $385 Rolex or my wallet full of documents and money. Certainly, an unconscious Caucasian can't be that common an occurrence. The explanation, I have always suspected, must lie somewhere between the usual African indifference to suffering (it is a part of their lives; they have no remedy for it; so why worry about it?), and a fear of being accused of causing my condition.

I told this story to an American friend recently, who commented, "Hell, that could have happened to you in New York City, and no one would have stopped to see what was wrong."

"Oh, yes they would," I countered, "I would have been mugged three times over before I woke up."

DINERS AND DINNERS:

As you can gather from the foregoing, African restaurants can be a true adventure, from the viewpoint of original meals, as well as the potential danger to life and limb. I ate in many native restaurants, from Morocco to Bulawayo, and was sick only once. One must, of course, observe certain precautions.

In North, West, or Central Africa, you should never eat foods that are not peeled or thoroughly cooked. Fresh, raw fruits and vegetables may have cholera or dysentery bacteria on their surface, as a result of inadequate sanitation or fertilizing with human feces. Do not drink unpurified water in these areas. Either refrain from drinking with your restaurant meals, or order something bottled—beer, soda, or what have you.

If you don't like taking chances, you can eat in your camper or tent from the native markets and stores. But try a restaurant now and then, just for the experience.

You can't really get the feel of a country and its people if you haven't sampled their food.

South African and Rhodesian restaurants are perfectly safe. In South Africa, Caucasians are prohibited by the policy of apartheid from eating with the natives— more's the loss. South African restaurants are quite expensive, much like American eateries, and are not much more exciting.

In East Africa, native and Indian restaurants are plentiful, the food is tasty and cheap, and the danger of infection is almost nonexistent. Here, you will often be presented with a choice of cow meat or goat meat with your meal. (The term "beef" is not commonly used.) If you are a trifle squeamish, ask for "ngombe", or cow meat. Feeling adventurous? Try the goat—it's not bad, really. In both East and South Africa, water and salads can be consumed with impunity.

FRESH FOODS:

Fresh fruits and vegetables are available everywhere, but the selection can be limited and rather boring. The foods vary considerably from region to region. By all means, shop for them in the native markets, which are often colorful and exciting, and give you your primary contact with the common people of the area. As an added bonus, you'll find fascinating non-food items—leatherwork, carvings, clothing, and other handicrafts.

Again, do not eat fresh fruits or vegetables that have not been peeled or cooked, when in North, West, or Central Africa. And don't wash your food in unpurified water to clean it. Fresh bread is available everywhere, and ranges from delicious to lousy-but-edible. Since it won't keep, you will rapidly learn to eat whatever is available.

We managed to get by with the unrefrigerated, but well insulated icebox that comes as standard equipment with a Volkswagen camper. Since all of Africa except the coastal regions is about a mile above sea level, it is seldom so hot that refrigeration is essential. Of course, it would be a welcome addition; you will undoubtedly spoil some food every now and then without it.

In Morocco, you'll be able to buy: tomatoes, onions, spices, carrots, delicious brown bread, cheese, green and red peppers, beef, and dirty rice. Oranges are a must at a penny apiece.

In the desert (Algeria and Niger) are: tomatoes, onions, dates, dirty rice, and bread with a taste like iron. (I never found out why; the water doesn't taste like iron.)

West Africa (Cameroun, Dahomey) offers: bread, pineapples, plantains, and bananas at about 25c for a bunch of 50. The bananas are delicious, the plantains not so hot. Vegetables are scarce, the peanut butter outstanding.

The Republic of Central Africa and the Congo provide: bread, bananas, occasional tomatoes, and not much else.

In the English-speaking countries (Rhodesia, South Africa, Uganda, Kenya, Tanzania, and Nigeria), almost anything you might want is available, even unto clean rice. Supermarkets abound in the more populous areas.

CANNED GOODS (AND SOME NOT SO GOOD):

Some canned goods are available everywhere, but quality and price vary widely. When you encounter high-quality goods at reasonable prices, try to stock up for several weeks, so you won't have to depend on the local supply.

Generally, the French-speaking countries (Morocco, Algeria, Niger, Cameroun, R.C.A., the Congo) have a very poor selection of tinned foods at exorbitant prices. A goodly percentage consists of damaged cans that are unsaleable in Europe. Never, never, never buy a can that is bulging outward; it may contain botulism or rotting food, and can kill you before you reach a doctor. Tins that are dented inward are usually safe.

By contrast, the English-speaking countries carry a much wider array of high-quality foodstuffs at reasonable prices. When in an ex-British colony, try to stock enough tins to carry you through the French countries into the next English one.

WATER CAPACITY:

Water is not nearly as scarce in the desert as petrol. Our capacity of 12½ gallons was more than enough for three people. However, we drove an air-cooled vehicle. A burst radiator hose or radiator leak in the desert could quickly consume your drinking water. You will need enough water for: drinking, cooking, washing dishes, bathing, replenishing your car's cooling system, and possible emergencies. You should always have sufficient water along to sustain the owner of the vehicle through three or four days of waiting with a disabled car while his caravan mates go for help. An abandoned vehicle is considered fair game for scavengers, and will be picked clean as a Christmas goose when you return for it. Suggested capacity: four gallons per person, plus the volume of your cooling system.

If you do not intend to cross the desert, carry a 10- or 20-liter can for emergencies. Water is always obtainable within the day's drive.

WATER PURIFICATION:

In South and East Africa, ordinary tap water is purified and drinkable. I drank filling-station water, just as I would in the States. In the desert, there is no surface water; all water comes from deep wells or underground streams, and is filtered naturally by the sand. It may at some places be cloudy and unappetizing, but is perfectly safe to drink. No precautions are necessary.

In West and Central Africa, watch out. Cholera, often transmitted through unpurified water, is a swift and merciless killer. Never, under any circumstances, drink unpurified water.

There are three methods of purifying your water: by boiling, filters, or pills.

Water is perfectly safe if brought to a boil, *then kept there for 15 to 20 minutes.* Unfortunately, this consumes an undue amount of time and effort, and is quite hard on the fuel supply for your stove.

Filters are available in Europe or Central Africa that are claimed to remove all harmful bacteria from water. It seems obvious that they are incapable of removing a nonfilterable virus. To my knowledge, no major intestinal disease is transmitted by such a virus; but, if you intend to rely solely on a filter, I'd suggest you first con-

Nigerian barbecue.

sult your physician, or better yet an expert on tropical diseases. The filter has the added advantage of removing dirt and cloudiness, so that your water is more palatable.

In Maradi, Niger, I purchased an Esser water filter, made in France, for about $4.40. It consisted of a ceramic cylinder, sealed at both ends except for a four-foot plastic tube at one end; it worked like a siphon. Each night, I would fill a bucket from the local water supply, and place it on the sink drainboard in the camper. The filter was placed inside. After the cylinder had become saturated with water, I would suck on the free end of the tube to start the siphon, and put it into a ten-liter water can on the floor. In the morning, I would have an entire can of clean water.

Other, similar filters can be found that are encased in a small hand pump. The water is pumped through the filter, forcing it through much more quickly than does the siphon. Of course, a great deal more effort is required.

Unwilling to trust the filter entirely, I added water purification tablets to the filtered water, at about two-thirds the recommended dosage. Pills are the simplest, surest method. Their only defects are that they don't remove dirt, and that you might run out far from civilization. By combining filter and pills, you are covered both ways, and can always resort to boiling in an emergency. The tablets are plentiful and inexpensive in America and East Africa. They are almost impossible to find right where you need them, in Central Africa.

There are three basic tablets on today's market: Iodine pills, used by the U.S. Peace Corps in Africa; dosage one tablet per quart; tastes awful. Halazone, a commercial U.S. product; one per quart; works fine, no taste. And Stereotabs, made in Great Britain and widely sold in East Africa; dosage one per liter; has a slight, but not objectionable taste.

If you should run out of pills, you can substitute tincture of iodine, commonly used for cuts and scratches. It should have a noticeable, but not overly strong, taste. Dosage: about four drops per quart. If you have no iodine, Clorox or any other liquid bleach will do the job. Just add one teaspoonful to eight gallons of water.

RAGS TO RAIMENT

South of Agadez, we came across a family of nomads living in goathide tents in barren desert country. We stopped to "talk", and discovered through sign language that two of their children were ill. Against my better judgment, John attempted to doctor them.

The younger children had hair cut in a most peculiar pattern. A large, oval patch on each side of the head was shaved bald. A strip of hair was left down the center, running from front to back, in the manner of the Mohawk Indians back home. Another strip remained, circling each of the ovals. We never did discover the purpose of this unique practice.

As John was administering whatever medications he had, the eldest child walked up. He was a lad of perhaps ten years, long and lithe, with wild, unshorn hair. His sole article of clothing was a leather thong across one shoulder, from which were appended four leather wallets. So far as we could determine, he owned no other clothing.

At the other extreme was John himself, who carried precious few belongings for his own comfort, but had half a duffel bag full of clothing to trade with the natives.

WHAT TO BRING AND WHAT TO LEAVE:

But what about your own clothes? What should you bring or leave at home? A few, simple rules should keep you out of trouble.

First, try not to bring anything you can't afford to lose. Expensive coats, sweaters, or jewelry are a liability. You have to worry about their getting lost or stolen, and you are flaunting your comparative great wealth before the locals.

This young man is wearing his every possession.

Used, casual clothes of a sturdy variety are best. Khakis, semi-dressy Levis, and sportshirts should comprise the bulk of your wardrobe. Neither new nor expensive, they should not be too ratty. You may spend some time in Europe, or in South Africa's comparatively dressy cities; and you'll have difficulty crossing some borders if you are not decently attired. One medium-weight sport coat and tie are sufficient for the few occasions on which you might need them.

As far as is practicable, everything you carry should be drip-dry or permanent-press, as you will undoubtedly wash them out by hand and hang them up to dry many times. Avoid all-polyester clothing, though; it does not breathe well, and will quickly become sticky and sweaty in hot weather. Dacron-and-cotton and some wool are best.

Avoid taking more than you can carry on your back. The more you have, the more you will have to launder, store, clean, and handle. You'll probably pick up a few items of handicraft along the way; so storage space will grow less rather than more. And, if you should have to abandon your vehicle and walk or hitch a ride onward, you'll want to leave behind as little as possible.

Be prepared for very hot and moderately cold weather. Short pants, swim trunks, a broad-brimmed hat, and sunglasses for the heat; warm sweater, heavy jacket, and wool sox for the cold.

A spare pair of sunglasses in case of breakage or loss is a good idea. Plastic glasses scratch way too easily for desert use; a good, glass lens is your best choice. Look for a pair marked "6-base lens", which indicates the number of separate polishings that the glass has undergone. Since you will be wearing them no less than twelve hours a day in the desert, it is silly to settle for anything of lesser quality.

Bausch and Lomb Ray Bans are expensive, but are the very best glasses available. They can be purchased for under $15 from: Klein's, 227 West Washington Street, Chicago, Illinois 60606; or Gander Mountain, P.O. Box 248, Wilmot, Wisconsin 53192. A cheaper pair will do for extras.

A handy accessory is a photographic lens brush, which can be bought in any camera shop for under a dollar. You will find it invaluable when your glasses become coated with red dust every thirty minutes, in parts of the Sahara. A small, good quality paint brush is a viable substitute.

You'll encounter rainy seasons. Bring a long poncho or a complete rainsuit. The Sears Roebuck catalog lists an all-nylon poncho for about $8.00. Here, you have a choice between: rubberized fabric, which is absolutely waterproof, but cannot breathe, so that you end up bathed in perspiration; and nylon, which leaks a little in a really hard rain, but breathes enough for comfort. The nylon is much lighter and more compact; and the nylon jacket doubles as a comfortable windbreaker.

Also recommended is a pair of water-resistant boots. Best in this line are European hiking boots, obtainable anywhere in Europe. They are best and cheapest ($10 to $20) in Germany. They will keep your feet warm and dry under almost any conditions; and you can walk as far as your legs hold up, if you have to. Don't buy the stiffer climbing boots, or the suede, rough-out kind, which soak up water like a sponge. Good boots can be bought in the U.S. at greater expense ($20 to $40) from

L. L. Bean, Freeport, Maine 04032; or Recreational Equipment, Inc., 1525 11th Avenue, Seattle, Washington 98122.

A pair of old combat boots will do in a pinch; but be prepared to have wet feet during the rainy season. If you expect to do any real hiking and can't afford good boots, bring a pair about a half size too large, and wear two pair of heavy, wool sox. The extra sox provide the padded give and added warmth that a pair of cheap boots lack. Whatever you do, don't rely on a pair of rubber boots for walking; they don't breathe, like the rubber rainsuit, and the soles are often too stiff to flex with your feet.

Some clothing is best purchased in Africa. Leather sandals are very inexpensive. Djellabas, ankle-length hooded robes, are ideal for desert wear. They can be had in any Moroccan market for $5 to $15, depending on your bargaining ability. Get the ones made from heavy wool for warmth during those chill, desert evenings.

Some bargains are also available in Europe for the careful shopper. German hiking boots are one example. I bought a goose down, mountain-climbing jacket for $30 at Black's of Greenock, in London. 100%-shetland-wool sweaters are sold in England for as little as $6. You'll have to do some looking, though; Europe isn't the bargain paradise she used to be.

A considerable volume of used, American clothing is for sale at ridiculously low prices in the native markets. We learned that these are the same clothes that you and others like you donate to charity in your own home town. They are shipped to Africa and given free of charge to Arab traders. The Arabs, competing with one another and having no investment, sell them for almost nothing to local traders, who operate in the village markets. These traders sell direct to the people.

When I first heard of this arrangement, I was incensed that clothing contributed to charity was given free to someone whose sole interest was to make a profit. Then I realized that it would cost far more to hire someone to transport the goods to remote villages, and then pay someone else to distribute them, than is expended on the small profits of the traders.

Prices are unbelievable. In Zinder, I bought a $9 pair of corduroy Levis for 60c; in Malawi, Phil Belanger, one of my several Canadian passengers, purchased a cashmere topcoat for one kwacha, or $1.40. It was thereafter referred to as his "kwacha coat". And we, I am sure, paid far more than the local people.

Despite this plentiful supply of inexpensive clothing, you will see some natives dressed in the most appalling rags—to the extent that, even after you had them laundered, you wouldn't use them to wipe a grease puddle off the garage floor. As might be expected, others are quite neatly dressed.

The list in Appendix VI will be more than enough to carry one male throughout the trip. Women should make appropriate substitutions.

Ladies: should you visit Malawi, be warned that both slacks and short skirts are illegal. Take one midi-length skirt (it must cover the knees); or buy a couple of yards of material in the local market for a few pennies, and drape it around your waist as a skirt. Don't let this one peculiarity frighten you off. Despite a strict moral code (or perhaps because of it), Malawi is in all other respects perhaps the most delightful country in Africa.

LUGGAGE:

The watchword here is "collapsible". Whatever luggage you bring should fold into a very small space when empty, so you won't have to find storage space aboard for it.

Most hitchhikers and many drivers use backpacks consisting of a rectangular, nylon bag, with separate, aluminum frame. These hold plenty of gear, are waterproof, collapse into a small space, and can be slung on your back if you have to walk out of somewhere or other. Features to look for are: outside pockets to hold small, often-used articles; long, 30" frame to hold sleeping bag beneath your pack; double-compartment design, with zipper all the way across, for easy access; over-sized, top flap to cover extras stuffed into the top of the pack; well padded shoulder straps; heavy nylon material for abrasion and water resistance; and heavy-duty fasteners that won't tear loose under strain. Chain discount stores now carry Japanese-made packs at bargain prices. For the deal of the year, visit your local Zayre: nylon bag with long frame, $14.99 and $19.99. No Zayre handy? Try Lionel Play World, $19.19; or your local army surplus store. Compare several before buying.

Cheaper bags, with integral frame or no frame at all, can be bought almost anywhere. They do not ride nearly as comfortably, and are not much good for long, cross-country hikes. For use as a suitcase, with only occasional backpack use, they might be a fair compromise, but will not deliver the best advantages of either.

If you don't feel the need for a backpack, consider duffel bags, hanging suit bags, soft-sided airplane flight bags, or anything else you may have that is made of canvas or other collapsible materials.

SEWING KITS:

Don't leave behind the old needle and thread. Even if you aren't in the habit of repairing your own clothing, you'll learn how on this trip. A sewing kit takes up very little room, and is invaluable when the seat of your pants rips open 250 miles from the nearest tailor. In the towns and villages, by the way, you will find competent and inexpensive tailors, who can manufacture anything from a shirt to swimming trunks.

Bring heavy-duty thread. Nylon is fantastically strong, but kinks up as you sew with it. Heavy, mercerized, cotton thread is a good alternative. A complete sewing kit is listed under *CLOTHING,* Appendix VI.

WHAT ABOUT
MEDICAL
CARE?

We came around a blind curve, cornering hard at about 40, the view ahead blocked by impenetrable, green foliage, growing to road's edge on either side. We were in Cameroun, an ex-French colony on the West coast of Africa, just below the great bulge of land that extends westward into the Atlantic. About fifteen miles ahead lay Yaounde, its capital city.

We were brought to an abrupt halt by a gaggle of vehicles and people cluttering the road. As we threaded our way past the confusion, we spied its cause—a young, black girl lying in the road, apparently a victim of an auto accident.

We stopped and stepped out amid three or four vehicles and twice as many spectators, to see if we could be of any help. One older man in particular seemed to be most concerned—a father or other relative, perhaps. I took a quick look at the girl, who was in serious need of help. She lay squarely in one lane of the road, obviously in a state of shock, quivering spasmodically and moaning softly. Her face was badly battered and swollen, her dress stained with crimson, and one leg twisted awry, about four inches of yellowish bone protruding.

In my execrable French, I tried to find out from the older man what had been done for her, whether anyone had gone for help, and what we could do to assist. He looked sorrowful and resigned, and shrugged eloquently. Unable to communicate effectively, I looked about for someone who spoke English. I was shocked to find that everyone had departed. No one stood ready to ward off traffic; nobody administered first aid; and, worst of all, no car had departed toward Yaounde, the only possible source of help.

We stood there a minute: I fretting silently; Rick Merry, my French-speaking, Canadian hitchhiker-of-the-month, doing his best to obtain some meaningful information; the old man repeating his explanation of how the accident happened and shrugging his shoulders in resignation. "Hell, Rick, let's go get an ambulance," I decided. "She needs a doctor badly; and we don't dare move her with that compound fracture. We might sever an artery, or something."

Jumping into the van, we took off hell-for-leather toward Yaounde, scrabbling around corners, hitting the potholes hard, making no effort to avoid the bad spots.

About five miles out of town stood a policeman directing traffic around a minor accident. We scrambled to a stop, backed up twenty feet, and spilled out our story in our best possible Francais. The policeman nodded, then shrugged placidly. "Elle est mort," he intoned calmly.

"Ne pas mort," I informed him, "ne pas." He smiled benignly, and shrugged once again.

We drove on. Soon we found what we were looking for: a white sign lettered in red, "HOPITAL". We followed the arrow, found it quickly, parked, and dashed inside. The man on duty carefully heard us out. "I'm sorry, this is a psychiatric hospital. We don't do that sort of thing. You'll have to go the the big hospital in town," he informed us.

"But that girl is lying there dying," I pleaded. "Can't you call them for us or something?"

"I'm sorry, this is a psychiatric . . ." We didn't wait to hear the rest, but ran for the van.

We reached the main hospital some minutes later, and went through our by now familiar routine. "That is not our concern," said the attendant. "That is a police problem."

Vaguely aware that a new presence had entered the room, I asked exasperatedly, "Can't you at least call the police and see if someone has sent an ambulance for her?" As he picked up the phone, I turned to the newcomer, a white-coated doctor. "At last," I thought, "we're getting somewhere."

"What seems to be the problem, gentlemen?" he asked in faultless English. We explained our predicament for the fourth time. "Oh . . . well, we don't do that; the police do that."

"Look, Doctor, I don't know anything about that. I only know there's this girl lying out there in the road, and no one seems to want to do anything about it. Can't you check with the police, and make sure . . ."

He cut me off. "Did you hit this girl?" he demanded.

"No, I'm just trying to . . ."

"What are you, American?"

"Yes."

"Well, then go to the American Embassy, and bother them about this. We're busy here; we don't have time to be bothered with you."

I pride myself that I managed to refrain from either verbal or physical retort. We left, shaking our heads sadly.

Medical care in Africa varies much as does the available food supply. It can be excellent, lackadaisical, or nonexistent. Should you require medical help in the desert, you will quite simply do without and ride it out on your own. Should you need it, as I did, in Zinder, or as that injured girl did, in Cameroun, you could suffer unaided within easy reach of a hospital. If you are fortunate, you will choose, as did Bjorn Enis, to get sick in one of the English-speaking countries.

Bjorn was a Norwegian journalist-student, whom we picked up in Yaounde. He stood about 6'6", and must have weighed all of 130 fully clothed. His face was surrounded by a shock of unruly red hair, and an equally unruly, equally red beard. Unfortunately, Bjorn was completely blind in one eye, and partially so in the other. He used to read avidly, holding the printed page about two inches from his good eye.

Perhaps because he couldn't just travel about and see his surroundings like the rest of us, Bjorn had truly "gone native". He was living in a filthy clay hut, in a run-down section of town, with nothing inside but a hard, dirt floor . . . and, oh yes, rats. He survived on manioc and bananas for a few cents a day, and drank any available water. His bare feet looked as if they hadn't been washed in months. It should not be necessary to add that of course he became ill.

His illness gradually worsening, Bjorn accompanied us through the Congo. After a long and wearing journey, we delivered him to a hospital in Fort Portal, a small town in Uganda. There, he was treated with the best of care, and fed far better food than he had had in months. I spoke to his doctor personally, and watched him work. I would have entrusted myself to him gladly. The hospital was spotless, the nurses busy and attentive. The only jarring note was the typically foul African toilet facilities, which apparently no one would clean up. After a ten-day stay, Bjorn's bill for room, board, doctor, and medication was about $30.

Moral: try to arrange to get sick only in the English-speaking countries. If that sounds a mite impractical, try taking all possible precautions, carrying a complete medical kit, and hoping for the best. Be as self-sufficient as you possibly can.

Unaccustomed to such luxuries as medical care, the true bush natives have a seeming resistance to pain that is startling. They are inured to sickness, injury, and death, with no medical help to alleviate the misery. They accept this as a natural state of affairs; while they don't enjoy it any more than you or I, they do endure it stoically.

I was told by some Norwegian volunteer workers in northern Uganda about the Acholi tribesman who walked into their hospital for treatment. He had been involved in some sort of local fracas, and had walked for three days afterward to get help, the splintered stump of a spear protruding from his abdomen.

SHOTS, PILLS, AND PRECAUTIONS:

There are several diseases to be guarded against while traveling. Some are prevalent only where sanitation is lacking, others only in the vicinity of carrying insects; some are a danger everywhere. A number of these can be avoided by taking shots, others with pills, some by appropriate sanitation and purification procedures. Almost all are readily avoidable.

The following is a comprehensive list of major health hazards, together with their most common cause and usual method of prevention. Should you contact any of these diseases, see a physician immediately.

1. Bilharzia: Also called schistosomiasis, bilharzia is caused by physical contact with a tiny parasite that resides in the body of a snail. Upon leaving the snail, it has approximately 48 hours to find another host. If you should happen to swim by during this time, you may be it. Prevention: don't. The snail is found in all still, fresh waters in Africa, with the sole exception of Lake Malawi. Confine your swimming and bathing to salt water, fast-moving streams, and Lake Malawi. If you fill your water cans from a lake or sluggish stream, be sure the water sits for over 48 hours or is boiled before you let it come into contact with your skin. Should you be exposed, early symptoms may not be noticed; you might not realize that the parasite is destroying your liver until several years have passed.

2. Cholera: the most vicious killer in Africa, cholera is characterized by continual diarrhea and vomiting—to the extent that, after about 48 hours of severe thirst, you will literally die of dehydration. It is transmitted by consumption of water or food that has contacted human feces. To prevent it, never consume unpurified water, or food that has not been peeled by you personally or thoroughly cooked. Protect all food from flies, and wash your hands thoroughly before handling food and immediately after defecating. Before leaving Europe or America, arrange to have the series of two cholera shots, one to two weeks apart, available at your local health service. Do not drop your guard after being inoculated; the shots are only 60% to 80% effective, and must be renewed every six months. Cholera is a danger only where sanitation facilities are inadequate. In East and South Africa, it is no problem; as usual, the French countries are the ones to watch. N'est-ce pas? While in Cameroun, I was privileged to read a Peace Corps doctor's rather whimsical poopsheet on this dread malady. "The difference between cholera and dysentery," the brochure explained, "is that, if you have to go to the john six or seven times a day, you have dysentery; if you can't get off the john, you have cholera." It shouldn't be necessary to tell you to see a doctor immediately.

3. Dysentery: Another intestinal disease, of two types: bacillary and amoebic. Both arise from consuming impure water or foods contaminated by human feces, and are characterized by more or less profuse diarrhea, often of a watery quality. Prevention is by observing the precautions described above for cholera. No immunization is possible. For treatment, the most common medication is Enterovioform, available at druggists everywhere in Africa, but recently removed from the U.S. market by the F.D.A. Other medicines are available on prescription from your doctor. Do not start your trip without several tubes; somebody in your party will undoubtedly need it. To stop up the symptoms without attacking the virus itself, take along a bottle of blackberry brandy; it works like the proverbial cork. Dysentery normally clears up spontaneously after several days or weeks.

4. Encephalitis: Caused by a virus transmitted through tsetse flies and occasional mosquitoes, sleeping sickness is indicated by inflammation of the brain, accompanied by chills, headache, and muscular pain. Respiratory or intestinal troubles may develop. Prophylaxis: don't get bitten. Buy mosquito netting and use

Friends. 6'6" Bjorn Enis with Congolese pygmy.

it; use Raid and Off to minimize insect contacts; cover up when in tsetse country (the Congo, and around the southern shores of Lake Victoria, among others).

5. Hepatitis: Also caused by contact with food or water contaminated by human feces, infectious hepatitis is typified by fever, nausea, and a sense of fatigue. Jaundice, a yellowing of the skin, may follow. Most patients recover in six to eight weeks. To avoid it, follow the precautions for cholera.

6. Malaria: Transmitted by the bite of a female anopheles mosquito, malaria is accompanied by fever, chills, and sweating. Recovery can be expected in ten to thirty days; but the attacks may recur periodically for years to come. Prevention is two-pronged: regular use of mosquito netting, insecticides, and repellents; and religious consumption of malaria-suppression tablets. Taken as directed, the pills should either prevent the disease, or reduce it to a sufficiently low level that its onset is not harmful. Malaria tablets are sold widely under such brand names as Resochin and Paladrin. Dosage as directed: daily, bi-weekly, or weekly. Begin taking the pills at least two weeks before entering a mosquito area, and continue for at least two weeks after leaving it. Treatment is by increased dosage of the preventive medicine, under a doctor's supervision.

7. Smallpox: This disease is caused by contact with an infected person or his clothing. Symptoms are chills, fever, and great fatigue; headache, backache, and muscular pain are optional; a red rash erupts on about the third day; death may result. Prevention is simple: be vaccinated before you go. There is no reason why you should become infected or require care. Vaccination is required by law before you may return to the U.S. anyway; simply have it done before you leave.

8. Snakebite: Perhaps the least likely health hazard you need worry about. The only snakes I saw during seven months in Africa were in the Nairobi Serpentarium. But, then, you never know... Prevention consists of keeping your eyes open, watching where you step, and not harassing snakes that are minding their own business. There are two types of poisonous snakes: pit vipers, which have triangular heads with two tiny, nostril-like holes, and whose poison is hemotoxic (transmitted through the blood stream); and neurotoxic snakes, whose venom attacks the central nervous system independently of the blood stream. Treatment for either type begins with killing the snake and bringing it with you so that its type can be identified. This should be followed by immediate administration of antivenin appropriate for that snake.

Antidotes can be purchased that are effective against all pit vipers, most neurotoxic snakes, or both; others work only against one particular species. If you wish even minimal protection, you should carry at least a snake-bite kit for pit vipers, plus mamba and cobra antivenins. Read instructions carefully before buying antivenins: some have a comparatively short shelf life; others require refrigeration, which may be impossible when traveling; most are made from horse serum, to which some people have severe allergic reactions—if allergic, make sure you get antivenin not made from horse's blood.

If bitten by a hemotoxic snake, further treatment is as follows: immobilize the bitten limb; pack in ice if you have any (an alternative is a small, spray can that can be used to cool tissue); avoid exertion; apply a tourniquet between the bite and your heart, but loosen it for one minute every half hour to release the poison into the system slowly, and to prevent gangrene; cross-shaped cuts across the fang punctures, followed by suction, are no longer recommended; find professional help.

If a full-grown, neurotoxic snake nails you with a full load of venom, you may well die within a matter of hours from respiratory failure. Get to a hospital or other source of antivenin any way you can. If you can't, avoid exertion, take nothing that might inhibit respiration (such as alcohol or morphine), grit your teeth, and pray.

9. Tetanus: Lockjaw, as it is commonly known, is indicated by strong muscular spasms, including those muscles that control the jaw. It is caused by a bacteria found in animal feces, which enters the body through wounds, small cuts, or insect bites. Prevention is by removing all foreign matter from the wound, promoting bleeding to drain it, and obtaining a shot of antitoxin as soon as possible afterward. The same injection may be taken as a booster shot before any injury occurs. Do not take the shot until you have determined that you are not sensitive to horse serum, as the allergic reaction can cause severe illness. Non-allergenic serums, called toxoids, are now available.

10. Typhoid: Like her sister disease, paratyphoid, this little beauty arises from contact with human feces through poor sanitation or improper food handling. Symptoms are chills, fever, backache, diarrhea or constipation, and headache. Bronchitis and rosy spots on the chest and stomach may be present. Occasionally, death results. Prevention is the same as for cholera. Before you leave, get the combined immunization that protects against both typhoid and paratyphoid, in a series of two or three weekly shots. Infection is unlikely, once you are inoculated.

11. Yellow Fever: Transmitted by the female Aedes Aegypti mosquito, this disease is accompanied by fever, possible chills, slow pulse, and flushed face. Control: be vaccinated before you go. With today's inoculation procedures, you will not become infected.

You needn't worry too much about any of these ailments, if you observe the proper precautions. See *Disease Prevention*, Appendix VI for a check-list.

YOUR FIRST AID KIT:

Commercially prepared medical kits can be bought almost anywhere in the U.S. or Europe. Most, however, are expensive and unsuited to the peculiar problems you may encounter. You can supplement such a kit or make your own, by following the *First Aid Kit* list in Appendix VI. Be sure to include eyewash and eyecup. The air in most parts of Africa is filled with a fine, abrasive dust, that can wreak havoc with the surface of the human eye. And don't forget to add anything you might need for personal medical problems. If you are subject to allergic reactions, carry antihistamine; if you wear eyeglasses, bring an extra pair; if you require regular medication of any kind, include a six-month supply.

You will be able to purchase most medical items in South or East Africa; not so in the West or North; even Europe can be lacking in things we take for granted. Highly recommended is Monks Pharmacy in Nairobi; if Ellis Monks doesn't have it, no one will. In Central and North Africa, the language barrier becomes almost insurmountable. How do you say "paratyphoid" in French?

Moroccan public bath.

UNSANITARY FACILITIES:

My first African rest room (an extremely loose use of the term) was at a restaurant in Ceuta. I was directed to a nearby door, and entered, pulling the door shut behind me.

It was a sub-closet-sized cubicle, about four feet wide and two deep. There was no light; it took several seconds to make out the surroundings. One stood with his back against the door and urinated on the wall, scant inches away. A foot-square hole chopped in the wall at eye level sufficed for both ventilation and light. A concrete gutter was built into the floor along the wall, to provide drainage to the street outside. That's it, folks. A fairly typical African toilet.

Most johns consist of a square hut, perhaps 4' by 4', with a concrete floor and a round hole cut in its center. That's all. One squats over the hole and lets fly.

This lack of vitreous china is not much of a loss. Once you have mastered the use of what is euphemistically referred to as the "Arab squat position", without dirtying your clothes or dragging your belt buckle through the mire, you will find it to be reasonably comfortable, versatile enough for any location, and completely antiseptic (you touch nothing).

Unfortunately, the same can't be said for the facilities themselves. They are almost invariably grimy beyond description. Africans apparently have some sort of compunction against scrubbing down a head—at least, they never seem to do it. As

66

there are no washing facilities, they simply wipe their hands on the closest wall—and there it stays for five or six years.

Recommended technique for combating the resulting odor is to breathe deeply several times before entering, so as to hyperventilate your lungs. Then enter quickly, and complete your business without delay. Postpone that first breath for as long as possible, and thereafter inhale as seldom and as shallowly as you are able.

After a while, you may well prefer to practice the Arab method while communing with nature in the great outdoors. The stance is identical, it is far more sanitary, and odor is not a problem. Don't worry too much about being seen. If the locals all do it, why can't you?

As previously mentioned, you will need to bring your own paper. Stock up before leaving the States, if you are not accustomed to using 220-grit sandpaper. Peel off a few yards in the morning, fold it into a small packet, and stick it in your hip pocket. It has a variety of other handy uses as well.

If all this makes you just a trifle squeamish, buy yourself a camping toilet, to be used inside your vehicle. It consists of an aluminum-framed, folding chair, much like a campstool. In place of a canvas seat, it has a plastic toilet seat; a plastic garbage bag, in the open position, clamps underneath. After use, simply tie off the mouth of the bag, dispose of it, and fold the unit up flat for easy storage. Cost: $4.99 at most camping equipment stores. I recently priced one at a nearby K Mart for $2.97. Bring *lots* of plastic bags.

Toilet facilities are much more acceptable in East Africa, and are quite clean and sanitary in the South. As usual, North, West, and Central Africa are the worst culprits.

About bathing. I showered under almost every conceivable set of circumstances: standing in the bush, with a one-gallon bucket to pour over me; in Arab bains, where you pour water on yourself from a tin can; outside a filling station, taking advantage of the only hose in town; and, upon occasion, just me, a cake of soap, and a rainstorm. Often, we settled for what the British refer to as an A.P.C. bath ("armpit and crotch") in the camper; and at times, when water was scarce, for no bath at all. You will, I am sure, quickly learn to do the same.

Once in a long while, you will be presented with what will seem like the opportunity of a lifetime—to cop a free shower from the Nairobi Hilton, or some such fancy establishment. The trick here is to walk in with an air of casual ownership, neatly dressed, and help yourself, just as if you were paying $35 a day for the privilege. Among other petty crimes I was led to commit, I stole showers in this fashion from some of the finest hostelries on the continent.

In Morocco, we befriended the security chief at the Rabat Hilton, and camped in perfect comfort and safety in the Hilton parking lot, not ten yards from the city's purest water supply. We utilized the hotel's men's room to the fullest (alas, no communal showers). I went so far as to wash my hair in the sink. There I stood, head covered with soapsuds, sloshing water over the immaculate tiled floor, when an official looking gentleman in a neatly pressed suit walked in. I nodded and smiled in friendly fashion, then ignored him completely. Well, at least they didn't throw us out.

BORDERS, VISAS & SUCH

Our first African border hassle was at our first African border—Morocco. We had been warned by young Americans in Spain that the Moroccans wouldn't admit "heads"—kids with long hair. This presented no problem to short-cropped me, but worried my two Canadians somewhat, since both had shoulder-length hair.

As we drove up to the border post, we were approached by an incredibly dirty Arab in ragged djellaba, who handed us entry forms and carried information from our car to the building, all under the disinterested gaze of the officials.

Each time he drew near the van, this paragon of impartial officialdom hissed, "Pelo, pelo!" in tones of deep conspiracy. On each such occasion, the mysterious admonition grew more insistent. After about the fifth or sixth repetition, it finally penetrated my lack of linguistic ability that our apparition was repeating the Spanish word "pelo", or hair. He was informing us, in his own inimitable way, that upon seeing those Prince Valiant haircuts in the van, the border officials would deny us entry. He pointed repeatedly at Boyd McBride in the back seat, proud possessor of the longest hair in sight, and then motioned for money. "Pesetas, pesetas," he demanded.

Boyd shook his head, fished a pair of scissors out of his gear, and made as if to begin cutting. Our Arab was horrified. "No, no," he protested vehemently, "pesetas, pesetas!" We had struck a nerve.

The border guards had a nice racket going. They couldn't care less whether an incoming tourist had long hair; but, if they kept a few heads out and scared a few more, word would spread, and soon all the kids entering Morocco would fork over

This fierce looking tribesman chased John Ibbotson around the camper—then broke into loud laughter.

a small bribe. Possibly no other entrant had so quickly and willingly indicated a preference to cut rather than pay. By dint of Boyd's intransigence, we ultimately paid a tip of only 50 pesetas, a considerable savings over the usual pelo bribe.

Each border crossing seemed to present its own little problem. Some were amazingly easy, others utterly exasperating. The difference often seemed to be determined by sheer chance.

VISAS:

Step number one is to obtain a visa. But where? If you want to find representatives of all countries in one place and deal with the highest possible caliber of official, apply in New York, London, or Paris. No other world capitals have more or better-staffed embassies. You will receive far more efficient treatment and less harassment. In New York or London, the language barrier will be all but nonexistent. There are two disadvantages. Many visas expire within three to six months, and may well be void by the time you arrive at the border. And you will have to leave your passport for a day or so with 15 to 20 different ambassadors, a time-consuming procedure at best.

If you apply in one of the African capitals, you may meet with less efficiency and more bureaucracy. For those countries not represented, however, visas are usually obtained through the British or French Embassy. This results in a minimum of mickeymouse and a considerable savings in time—you leave your passport with only two different embassies for eight or ten entry permits. We obtained the great bulk of our visas in this manner in Rabat, Morocco. If proceeding from south to north, wait until you reach Lusaka, Zambia, or Nairobi. Rhodesia and South Africa are anathema to most black African officials, because of their racist policies.

Some countries may not have representation in all capital cities. Some may refuse you entry. Don't be discouraged; try each embassy you encounter until you get what you are after. Upon occasion, you may find that the consulate in the next neighboring country, or even the border station itself, is your best or only chance of success.

Forget about applying by mail before you leave. By the time you mail your passport to New York and back 15 times, your first visas will have expired and your passport will reside peacefully in someone's dead letter office.

The procedure begins with presenting yourself at the embassy with valid passport, health certificate, and three passport photos. Ask for the visa, and try to find out what length visas are available at what cost. Some officials are cagey about this. They may sell you a thirty-day entry permit for $5, when a fifteen-day one at $2 will do; or they may issue a twenty-day visa, when ninety days are available at the same price. Try to figure in advance the length of time you might wish to stay in each country, but always get the maximum available time without paying a fee increase. Costs vary. We paid from $2 to $11 each in Rabat and Yaounde.

Be prepared for writer's cramp. At the French Embassy in Rabat, we each filled out 15 legal-sized forms printed on both sides—in French. After scribbling at top speed for a full ninety minutes, we left them behind with 15 passport photos and 55 dirham (about $11) apiece. After three or four days, my fingers opened and closed almost normally.

You will have to surrender your passport and return later. Waiting periods vary from a half hour to three days for each visa. The U.S. Government advises that you demand a receipt each time you leave your passport with someone, to protect against its loss, and to explain its absence should you be questioned by police. We found this advice to be impractical. The various African officials considered such a request to be an impertinence, and declined to write out a receipt. We left our passports at many different embassies with never a loss.

If you do the entire transcontinental trek, your passport will rapidly fill to overflowing with multiple visas. Any U.S. Embassy will provide you, free of charge, with an accordion-style, foldout insert for additional stamps. No hurry—you can get one whenever you run out of room.

HOW TO CROSS BORDERS:

Border officials should be regarded as your friends and equals. Be neither condescending nor fawning; do not show irritation or impatience. Some officials may go out of their way to make things difficult for you. Often, their sole purpose is to force you to acknowledge that they are in control of the situation. They have been pushed around by Whitey long enough. Solution: give in gracefully, and ask for the aid of their superior knowledge in straightening things out.

Speak some French if you are able; but make clear the limitations of your ability. To refuse to try French at all is rather arrogant; to nod politely to sentences you don't understand could lead to all sorts of complications. If your French is limited, go through the greetings and small talk in French, then explain laughingly that your Francais is "tres mal, M'sieu', tres mal." Smile and don't sweat it. It will all come out all right.

A fluent interpreter is a big help. I had trouble getting the van into several countries for lack of the proper documents, only to have Captain Deb or another French-speaking friend smooth things over in a matter of seconds.

OBSTACLES AND BRIBES:

There are several countries which present border problems. Possibly the worst of all is Nigeria, where bribery, called "dash", is a national institution.

We had been warned that the Nigerian Government was incensed by American newspaper support of the Ibo rebels during Nigeria's civil war. In retaliation, American citizens were denied access to the country, even for purposes of transit. Unfortunately, it is almost essential to traverse the country to reach East, or even Central Africa.

We presented ourselves at the Nigerian Embassy in Rabat with little hope. The consul, a stocky, round-faced black, received us brusquely. "No, you may not have visas. My country's policy is to refuse admission to all Americans. . . . Yes, I understand that there is no alternate route to East Africa. . . . No, you may not have 48-hour visas just to pass through; nor 24-hour visas either. . . . No, I have no other suggestions. I can not offer you any help whatever." We left in utter defeat.

Undaunted, we headed south from Morocco, mulling over the possible alternatives on the way. We could try for a visa at the Nigerian Embassy in Niamey, Niger;

fat chance. Failing that, we could brace several of the smaller border stations in the hope of talking our way through one; this seemed well worth a try, but offered small hope. Or, we could sneak through the northeast corner of Nigeria on a rough track that had no border station; we were warned, however, that we might be attacked by bandits or arrested, in either event risking loss of the camper. A fourth possibility was to circumvent the country entirely, via an all-but-impassable sand waste extending around Lake Chad; this route was so rough and so unused that the risk of losing the van became a near certainty. Last chance: go to Cotonou, Dahomey, on the west coast, in hopes of catching a freighter to Central or South Africa; this entailed a wait of up to six months and a possible cost of up to $500. Only the first two alternatives seemed to make much sense.

In Maradi, Niger, we got lucky. A friend of a friend of a casual acquaintance turned out to be the local police chief. This worthy gave us a note to the Niger border post, which sent a messenger to the Nigerian border station at Jibiya. The official there gave us a 48-hour permit, good solely for travel to Kano, the capital, to apply for a visa.

Naturally, there was a hitch. The customs inspector, a beefy, pretentious individual, talked with us at some length. I did not, it appeared, have a "carnet du passage in douane" covering the VW. The only real help he could be was to offer to change some money for us. No? Well, the problem was that we didn't have the proper papers. Well, a temporary import permit raised certain difficulties. Were we sure we didn't want some money changed to facilitate our travel through his country?

We were dead sure. The official exchange rate was seven Nigerian shillings to one U.S. dollar. On the black market, we could obtain eleven to one, thereby increasing our purchasing power by over 50%. We declined politely.

The net result of this tactical error was that I was forced to leave the van and all my belongings at the border station, travel 233 miles to Kano in Ed Everts' Land Rover, and obtain a directive from the chief customs inspector instructing my persecutor to issue a temporary importation permit "on form X44". We were also fortunate to receive four-day visas to travel through Nigeria to the southeast, exiting through a specified point.

I returned to the border on a native bus, its handmade wooden body jammed with humanity, driven at top speed by a perpetually grinning, devil-may-care driver. I was privileged to pay 60c extra to ride in comparative comfort on the hard, wooden, front seat with the driver and six other passengers—that's right, eight in the front seat. The return trip consumed a mere ten hours.

I once again braced the recalcitrant customs official. Yes, he understood the note from Kano; but he thought he had run out of form X44. He could, however, be of help to me by cashing some dollars. The light dawned. I fished out a $20 bill, rejected his offer of six shillings to the dollar, and accepted seven, the bank rate. He disappeared for twenty minutes to "get change"—more likely, to lay off my $20 on a black marketeer at eleven to one.

Within about two minutes after allowing myself to be taken for the eighty shilling difference in rates, I was on my way. For a lousy $7.20, I could have saved myself two days of discomfort and uncertainty.

Whether you wish to distribute dash or not I leave to your individual conscience. But in either event, listen for suggestions that seem out of place in your conversation with a border official. They may at least tell you what he has in mind.

Start trying for your Nigerian visa early. London is a good spot to begin; Niamey, Niger, is probably your best bet; try every border station you come to as a last resort. Your chances are probably better if headed from south to north; for some reason, officials in Nairobi and Lusaka are less uptight about the whole thing than those in the north. Whatever you do, don't profess an interest in journalism, the Ibos, or southwestern Nigeria.

There are other problem countries. The Democratic Republic of the Congo drags its feet, but will issue a visa if you persist. This huge chunk of primitive real estate is usually called Congo (Kinshasha) after its capital, to distinguish it from its sister state, Congo (Brazzaville). It was recently renamed Zaire by President Mobutu, to emphasize the break from its European-dominated past. Watch this one. The consul may sell you the standard, $11 visa, when an eight-day, transit visa is available for $2. Decide which you want and ask for it.

Several African nations will refuse admittance if you have lived in or even visited countries with whom they do not get along. Congo (Kinshasha) will deny you entry if you have a Congo (Brazzaville) permit. The only feasible route from North to East Africa is through Congo (Kinshasha). If this is your destination, better skip Brazzaville. Congolese or other Central African officials may balk at the sight of a Belgian or Portugese visa obtained on a trip through Europe; this cannot be too serious a problem, as I was never once questioned about the Portugese stamp hidden amidst about 100 others in the inner recesses of my passport. Egypt will positively deny admission if you have been stamped in and out of Israel. And more than one black country will keep you out if you have been through Rhodesia or South Africa.

There are four possible solutions to this problem: plan your trip so as to avoid any offending nations, or so as to visit them last; request that your entry permit be stamped on a separate piece of paper so that it can be removed later (I am told that Israel at least will do this); apply at any U.S. Embassy for a new passport (you may have to turn in your old one); or obtain the offending stamps on the end sheet of your accordion foldout (since the pages are unnumbered, you can subsequently cut off the last fold or two). This last is extremely illegal and could conceivably result in forfeiture of your passport.

If you do travel through Rhodesia or South Africa, get a tourist visa rather than a working permit. The former is much less offensive to black officials elsewhere.

South Africa and Rhodesia may require display of sufficient funds to pay for an airplane ticket all the way to your home country. The amount involved can be several hundred dollars. Several outs are available: carry $500 or so extra in travelers checks; take a letter of credit from your local bank stating that you have ample funds on deposit; or keep a refundable airline ticket, open as to date, for your return home.

One of my Canadians pulled an increasingly common stunt. He informed American Express that his $1,000 in travelers checks had been stolen, and obtained an additional $1,000. The second batch he spent traveling; the first $1,000 was used solely to show the Rhodesian and South African border guards. Not wishing to actually defraud anyone, he then destroyed them. Unfortunately, many of today's kids, oriented toward the rip-off and scoring on Ma Bell, are even less honest, and sell the "stolen" checks on the black market. Obviously, any such behavior constitutes fraud and perjury. One of these days, American Express is going to grow weary of being scored on, and will put someone in the penitentiary for about five years. I wouldn't recommend being the guy who is playing fast and loose with them at that moment.

This and other border problems are far less likely if you appear to be a reasonably substantial citizen. Ownership of a decent looking vehicle helps; freaky paint jobs or junky appearance will hurt. As you approach a problem border, stop, clean up, and put on halfway respectable clothing. Youth, unduly long hair, unkempt beards, ragged clothing, and outlandish costumes are all likely to cause difficulties.

Some countries are impossible or impractical to cross. Egypt will allow you to pass through by plane or train, but your vehicle must ride a boxcar. No driving about looking at military installations. Countries involved in civil war or insurrection are extremely dangerous—stay out. When we were in Africa, the Sudan was impassable for this reason. Such situations change from time to time. Ask lots of questions, and keep your ears open. Travelers bound in the other direction are a goldmine of information.

Be wary of countries that have undergone recent military coups or power struggles. Uganda, a beautiful and otherwise delightful nation, had undergone just such a coup shortly before our arrival. The army were in control, and were answerable to no one but themselves. Suspected enemies of the state might suddenly drop from sight on a more or less permanent basis.

While in Fort Portal, we heard shots in the night, followed by an ominous silence. We learned later that the local police chief had been arrested by the military, and was shot for "resisting" or "escaping" on the way to jail. His crime: he was suspected of being opposed to the new regime—because he was born a member of the same tribe as the recently deposed president. Once inside the local prison, we were told, prisoners were quite safe and reasonably well treated. It was getting there in custody of the military that was dangerous. The jail had earned the nickname, "University of Discipline", to reflect the number of intellectuals and educated politicians housed there.

The potential danger was dramatically confirmed late one night in Kampala's native quarter, where we had dropped off one of our two black African passengers. We were run off the road by a Jeepload of inebriated soldiers armed with rifles and automatic weapons. The leader, his breath reeking of alcohol, demanded angrily, "What you do here? Me think you spy-ers. You spy-ers." Another, eyes glazed, pointed a semi-automatic rifle unsteadily at my head. A third dragged our Ugandan friend out of the van to ascertain, "What you do here? Why you bring these people here?"

We produced our passports at the leader's request. He carefully examined Bjorn Enis' upside down. "Oh, well," I thought, "It's an English-speaking country. He'll be able to read mine." I watched in numbed disbelief as he inspected it sideways.

After several more accusations of "Me think you spy-ers" and denials of "Oh, no, man; I'm just an American tourist", we were set free, shaken but unharmed. It occurred to me only afterward that the entire, nightmarish scene was probably a shakedown—that a $10 bill would have smoothed things over in a hurry. My mind works a little slowly in that direction sometimes.

Some nations have cute, trick regulations. Tanzania requires a special license for a "foreign commercial vehicle", which is liberally interpreted to include VW vans and other cars large enough to carry passengers for hire. You must go out of your way to purchase it before you reach the border (at the Tanzanian consulate in Nairobi if preceeding south; in Zomba, Malawi, or Lusaka, Zambia if headed north). No one will mention it at the border as you enter. We met one American tourist in a VW camper, who was fined $300 as he left for failure to have one.

Algeria has a system of issuing gas coupons to tourists, so that they can save part of the high fuel cost in the desert. Ask for the necessary forms when you get your visa. We failed to do so, could not get forms at the border, and paid up to $1 per gallon as a result.

Algeria and other countries require that you buy compulsory auto liability insurance as you enter. They will not accept any existing insurance you may have, unless it is issued by one of a few specified companies. While this is a bit of a racket, it is best to pay and forget it. It could save you from arrest or confiscation of your vehicle if you should have an accident (unlikely though that may seem on a little-traveled sand track).

FRONTIER POSTS:

On entering the sand-track portion of the Sahara, you will be required to pass a frontier post. The officials here will be concerned, not with visas and documents, but with tools and equipment, fuel and water capacity, first aid kits and spare tires. If you are reasonably well equipped, you should have no trouble. You may be required to wait to convoy up with other vehicles. Do so cheerfully; it is in your best interests.

DON'T OVERLOOK UNCLE SAM:

You will, of course, have to clear U.S. Customs on your return. Here you will need your passport, health certificate showing a current smallpox vaccination, and receipts for anything purchased overseas. If you bring your vehicle back, you should have its registration and bill of sale, a statement of origin, and a receipt for steam cleaning the underside shortly before leaving Africa. Steam cleaning is required by U.S. Customs, to destroy crop pests that have been known to hitchhike into the country on someone's differential housing. It can be done on arrival in the States, but will be more expensive and may cause considerable delay. The statement of origin is an affidavit signed by the manufacturer of a vehicle built overseas. It establishes compliance with U.S. safety specifications.

Before starting out, sort through your gear. Everything made outside the U.S. should be taken to the nearest customs office and registered. The registration slip is your proof that you do not owe duty on all that camping and photographic equipment that you lugged all the way to Africa and back.

SANITATION CONTROL:

Upon leaving cholera-stricken Cameroun and entering the Republic of Central Africa, we encountered something called a sanitation control station. It consisted of the usual straw hut, manned by an officer and two soldiers, charged with the duty of keeping contaminated food and water out of the country. We dumped all of our water and a goodly number of pineapples, but through some quirk of logic were spared a huge bunch of bananas. When Captain Deb and Superboot came through the same station about an hour later and reported no pineapples beside the road, we decided that the officer preferred pineapples to bananas for his breakfast.

Unless you visit an area undergoing some form of epidemic, you will never encounter this problem. If you do, the loss of some water and fresh food won't do you any harm.

MARY JANE:

One of the few places on earth where marijuana is more prevalent than in the U.S. is the entire continent of Africa. The stuff is cultivated almost everywhere, and is used in one form or another by most tribes. Nevertheless, many countries have criminal laws against its use. If you do indulge, you take your chances. One chance you needn't take is to try smuggling it across anybody's border. The stuff is so readily available and so cheap in the next country, anyway, that it just isn't worth the risk, however slight, of a few months in an African jail. Particularly paranoid on this subject are officials in South Africa and Rhodesia, who regard anything smacking of liberalism as an outright crime. The Rhodesian police have gone so far as to prosecust University of Rhodesia students for possession of mircoscopic particles found in their clothing.

Don't say you haven't been warned.

DOCUMENTS:

A SHORT COURSE

IN FORGERY

African officials may impose technical barriers to your progress almost whimsically; on other occasions, they may do so with good cause. In either case, a valuable weapon to have in reserve is an ultra-official-looking, though meaningless, document, with numerous stamps, ribbons, and seals. The less decipherable, the better.

I met an American peace corpswoman in Victoria, Cameroun, who had this problem taped. Someone had once given her in jest a fanciful certificate proclaiming her to have attained the rank of Admiral in the Navy of Nebraska. It was hand lettered in old English script, and fairly dripped ribbons and seals. According to all reports, this meaningless piece of paper had solved virtually every paperwork problem she had ever encountered.

I myself carried an insurance certificate issued in Germany. It had long since expired, and in any event was valid only in Europe and Morocco. However, it was several pages long and very formal looking, and was printed entirely in German. It was totally incomprehensible to me or anyone else. It baffled every official I showed it to, many to the point where they shrugged and backed down.

If you have no such document handy, or need papers referring to a specific problem or lack of documentation, explain your situation to the nearest U.S. Ambassador. In all probability, he will agree to prepare an affidavit for you to sign, stating whatever facts you wish to emphasize, to be signed by you under oath. This paper is absolutely worthless for any legitimate purpose; but it appears quite formal. It is typed on U.S. Embassy stationery, bears the Great Seal of the United States, is notarized by an Embassy official, and can be capped off with an impressive gold seal. In addition, it describes your automobile, passport, or other specific problem, and says whatever you want to say about it. With a little imagination, you can produce a real hummer. Most officials in French-speaking countries won't be able to read it anyway.

REQUIRED DOCUMENTS:

In addition to phony papers, you will, of course, require legitimate documentation. First and foremost is a current passport, which is issued by a passport agent located in any one of several major U.S. cities, for a period of five years. Submit your application, together with two identical passport photos, a certified copy of your birth or naturalization certificate, and a fee of $12. Application forms can be obtained from a passport agent, clerk of a federal or state court, or postal clerk. Check under "U.S. Government" in your phone book. You may apply by mail only if you have been issued a passport within the past eight years.

You will also need a visa stamped into your passport by an embassy of each country to be visited. See Chapter Nine for detailed instructions. Don't forget to take along 25 or 30 extra passport photos—most countries require three for each visa.

A health certificate, or "shot card", is essential. This is a small, yellow folder, containing a record of all your shots and inoculations. It is available free from any doctor, hospital, or health service that gives you shots, and can be added to as you go along. It must reflect at least cholera, smallpox, and yellow fever protection. Typhoid-paratyphoid is highly recommended. See Chapter Eight for details.

Helpful, but not necessary, is a student card, showing you to be a student at any school anywhere. If you can wangle one, you will receive reduced rates at student hostels, on airlines, and elsewhere.

Vehicle owners should carry both registration and certificate of title. In Europe, these two documents are combined into one international registration certificate. If registered in the U.S., bring both. Be sure the name on the vehicle papers matches that on your passport.

Drivers are required to have an international driver's license, obtainable from your local A.A.A. office. Submit your application with a valid, state driver's license, two passport photos, and a $3 fee. If you leave the U.S. without, it can be had almost anywhere in Europe.

Next is an insurance "green card", attesting that you have insurance against liability and property damage. Purchase such insurance covering every African nation before you go, if you can find it. Neither the A.A.A., Lloyd's of London, nor any of the several major companies I checked before leaving were of any help at all. Nor was I able to find any in Europe. After returning, when I no longer needed it, I located coverage written through American International Underwriters, 2355 South Salzedo Street, Coral Gables, Florida 33134. Policies are issued by American Home Assurance Company and Firemen's Insurance Company of Newark, New Jersey, both of 102 Maiden Lane, New York, New York 10005.

I was quoted the following rates on a $3,000 VW camper, for nine months in all African countries: $250,000 liability and property damage, $160; collision, $127;

comprehensive, $85. The $250,000 is a minimum requirement, and is limited to secondary coverage above the minimum limits of compulsory insurance required at some borders. With the compulsory insurance, you are fully covered. If you have an expensive vehicle, the comprehensive clause is the only known way to cover its theft. The only alternative to such a policy is to buy new insurance at each border, and, if that is unavailable or worthless, be a self-insurer. At any rate, carry with you an insurance policy of some sort describing your vehicle, no matter how invalid it may be.

If you should have an accident without liability insurance, you may well be arrested and imprisoned or have your vehicle impounded, pending the payment of damages. If covered by insurance, you will be patted on the back and sent on your way.

Equally important is a "carnet du passage in douane," which consists of a bond, posted by an automobile club, guaranteeing the government of each country you pass through that you will take the vehicle out of the country when you leave or pay the import duty. If you fail to do so, the issuing club is liable for the amount of the duty, which may be as high as $2,000 or more. It is all but impossible to cross certain borders without a carnet.

FORGERY MADE SIMPLE:

Not having had the benefit of this book, I arrived in Morocco without ever having heard of a carnet. Superboot clued me in, to my utter mystification. Asking around produced a great deal of confusing misinformation. One thing was certain— I would never gain entry to the Congo or East Africa without one, not to mention a round half dozen countries in between.

I started scrambling. Among other flailings about, I flew to Gibraltar, home of the nearest Royal Auto Club. Since my car was not registered in Gib, no soap; cost of re-registration there: prohibitive. We tried the Moroccan Auto Club: same story. I wrote my law partner in the U.S., asking him to try through the A.A.A. We moved on, hoping to meet his answer in Cotonou, Dahomey.

We talked our way into Algeria and Niger with no real difficulty. At the Nigerian border, I lost two days' time, a little dash, and a good deal of composure. (Read all about it in Chapter Nine.) Cameroun admitted me only after French-speaking Captain Deb smoothed the troubled waters. We never reached Cotonou, nor received an answer from the U.S. (My mail somehow got misplaced.) Happily, a passing German told me how and where to contact A.D.A.C., the German auto club. I wrote them and kept moving, expecting their response in Bangui, Republic of Central Africa. R.C.A. let us in after a little deception and trickery on our part. At Bangui, no mail yet.

Now we were really stuck. The next two countries were the Congo and Uganda, both absolute sticklers for a carnet. Rumors abounded: we could bribe a Congolese official; we could post a $2,000 bond and perhaps never get it back; we could have a local printer print a phony. One thing we could not do was to turn around and drive 5,000 miles back through all that rock and sand. We had to find a way.

My strong suit has always been honesty and straight dealing. In twelve years of law practice, I had never once done anything that was not upright and aboveboard all the way down the line. But the thought of turning around and going back after all we had been through was a little too much. I became a forger.

For $25, I bought the rear cover and six inexplicably blank pages from the back of an old carnet in the possession of some passing Australians. We then borrowed a typewriter and typed in all the pertinent information about my van, just as if it had been issued to me in the first place. To allay suspicion, we detached the two coupons on the top page, leaving the usual stub. This stub needed entry and exit stamps for Cameroun, R.C.A., or some other recent country.

Now the artistry began. We dated and signed ourselves in and out, using two different hands, and stamped the entry with a borrowed rubber stamp reading "Henri's Chemiserie"—smeared just enough to be illegible. The exit was beautifully sealed by applying a fifty-franc coin to the ink pad and then to the stub, followed by a slight twist for smear. A masterpiece! To my career of displaying false documents, black marketeering, and bribery of public officials, I had now added forgery.

This falsified beauty got us safely through the next three borders to Nairobi, where A.D.A.C.'s response caught up with us. Despite the fact that I had sent them $27 too little, they had issued a carnet to a complete stranger from a foreign country and mailed it off to the middle of Africa with a bill for the balance due. Nice people!

The carnet can be issued only by an automobile club in the country in which your car is registered. If you wish to save yourself untold grief, do not leave that country without your carnet. In the U.S., the nearest A.A.A. office will issue it; in the United Kingdom, look up the local branch of the A.A. (Automobile Association) or R.A.C. (Royal Automobile Club); if your registration is German, A.D.A.C. (Allgemeiner Deutscher Automobil-Club) is extremely helpful.

Cost varies from about $30 to $50. In addition, you may have to post cash bond or other security of up to $2,000, to protect the club. A.D.A.C. now has a non-refundable, lump-sum fee of DM75 (about $20) to replace this security. Whether others will follow suit is questionable.

As you enter each country, your entry is stamped onto the stub portion of a separate page, and a coupon from that same page is removed and retained by Customs. Upon leaving that country, you must take the initiative to see that the remaining coupon on that page is torn off and your exit stamped on the stub. The exit stamp is your proof that you removed the vehicle from the country and do not owe the duty. When you return the unused portion of the carnet to the issuing club with all used stubs marked with an exit stamp, they will return your security.

East Africa (Kenya, Uganda, and Tanzania) have formed a customs union, similar to a common market, so that you can travel from one to another of these countries without going through customs. Here, you have your carnet stamped in when you enter the first of the three, and obtain an exit stamp only when you leave the last.

MONEY AND THE

BLACK

MARKET

My introduction to black marketeering took place in Nigeria, and is described in Chapter Nine. After leaving our acquisitive border official and driving to Kano, we simply stopped at the first sizable roadside market, and asked about changing money. We were promptly directed to a local money changer, and received eleven shillings to the dollar, a clear profit of 57% over the official rate of seven to one. Does wonders for your purchasing power, and is only slightly dangerous.

An illegal market in currency arises because some countries restrict the export of funds by its citizens, or peg the official exchange rate at an unrealistic figure. Since, for instance, Kenyan shillings cannot be exported legally, they are not traded in Switzerland, London, or other centers of finance. A merchant or person of property living in Kenya may wish to sneak some money out of the country and into a Swiss bank, or send it home to India. Since Kenyan shillings are worthless there, he must have pounds or dollars, and he must compete for them with all others wishing to do the same. Competition swiftly outstrips the rate paid under official decree by the banks.

The more stable the foreign currency, the higher the price. I traveled in Africa shortly before U.S. devaluation. At that time, the dollar was king, and brought the highest price. Since devaluation, the British pound may be supreme. At last report, the German mark was running a poor third. Check before you leave, if possible; otherwise, hedge by taking pounds and dollars.

Where to find it? Simplicity itself: in Central African countries, just go to the nearest native market and ask where you can change some money. When introduced to the Man, ask him what rate he is willing to pay. It is unnecessary to suggest anything illegal. If you are in East Africa, try any Indian shop. (Virtually all shops there are owned by Indians, virtually all of whom seem to be named Patel.)

Countries with no currency restrictions generally have no black markets. In such nations as South Africa, Rhodesia, Malawi, and Morocco, you will obtain no advantage. Some countries with thriving black markets are: Nigeria, 11 to 1, bank rate 7 to 1; Uganda, 10 to 1, official rate 7 to 1; Kenya, 9 to 1, also officially 7 to 1; Egypt, 80 to 1, against 43 to 1 at the bank. Black markets also operate in Algeria and the Congo—exact rates unknown. Shop around; you'll find out.

A word of caution: dealing in currency at illicit rates is against the law. If caught, you might well be expelled from the country or arrested; the national with whom you were dealing may go to prison. If you do engage in such activities, you take your chances.

GOOD OLD AMERICAN EXPRESS:

Travelers checks are a two-edged sword. They are excellent protection against loss or theft, on the one hand, as American Express will replace them free of charge. On the other hand, they bring less than cash on the black market, and they do cost money. You are charged 1% when you buy them, and may pay an additional 1% to 3% commission when you cash them at an African bank.

Buy American Express rather than some other brand. They are far more widely accepted by banks and money changers alike. More important, American Express has an office in every major African city, where you can cash your checks sans commission, report their loss or theft, pick up your mail, and meet fellow Americans. No other check issuer offers such service.

What denominations to carry? Some large and some small: $100's and $50's for the countries in which you may stay awhile, and $20's and $10's when you are just passing through or are about to leave after a long stay. Try not to cash more than you expect to use. If you aren't careful, you'll find that you have paid 1% to buy the checks in the U.S., another 2% to cash them into, say, Moroccan dirham, and a third commission to change the dirham into Algerian dinars. Gets expensive after awhile. A few countries, such as Algeria, won't even let you take excess money out or change it into another currency. Makes a nice bonfire, though. Obviously, carrying all $100's would cost you money; all $10's are too bulky to carry.

You'll want to carry some cash, too, despite the risk of loss. It brings more on the black market, is great for bribes and dash, and is instantly convertible into local currency. A good mix might be $1,500 in travelers checks, $250 in U.S. dollars, $250 in British pounds, a letter of credit for $500 or so, and some personal checks.

You might consider purchasing an American Express credit card. For $15 per year, you can cash personal checks at any American Express office in the world for up to $50 cash or $450 in travelers checks. This privilege may well spare you from two or three weeks of waiting while a local bank clears your check through New York.

CHECKS: A LESSON IN FUTILITY:

Cashing a check in Africa is quite a scene without American Express.

If you are not so blessed, you must visit an office of the largest banking chain in the country—say, Barclay's in Nairobi, probably the most reliable of all African banks. There, you will be told that the bank will accept your check, but must clear it through a New York clearing house and your stateside bank before payment is made. They will cable, of course, and request a cabled reply to save you time. It may take as long as ten days or two weeks.

If your experience is anything like mine, after the initial ten days, you will present yourself daily at the bank until three to four weeks have passed—or however long it takes until you blow your top. You will be told repeatedly that they are very inefficient in New York, that Barclay's has cabled again (at your expense) to find out what is wrong, and that your funds will surely arrive tomorrow.

When you finally explode and demand an investigation, you'll discover that (a) the money has been received, but was inadvertently posted to "uncollected funds" (b) Your proceeds have been sent to the wrong branch of Barclay's (c) the dollar has been under heavy pressure, and the government has put a hold on all foreign transactions, or (d) all of the above. Your cost for the entire transaction: perhaps 1%, plus $10 to $15 in cable charges. Travelers checks are far, far simpler. (The above example should be construed as a comment on African banking generally, rather than on Barclay's, which is an excellent chain.)

While in Spain, I successfully left a check for collection at a branch bank in Madrid, and collected the proceeds at another branch in Malaga. The same procedure seems technically feasible in Africa, but is hardly recommended. For openers, most countries have only one large city, so that other branches within the same country might be few and far between. To request delivery in a neighboring country would run afoul of any currency restrictions, and cost you additional commissions for changing your dollars into first one, then another currency. Besides, if they can manage to lose your money so unfailingly within a single bank, I shudder to contemplate the chaos that could result from a multi-branch transaction.

CURRENCY CONTROL:

At the Algerian border, we were required to fill out a form listing all travelers checks and items of currency from any country, plus all objects of gold and photographic equipment. After carefully copying body and lens numbers from my camera and telescopic lenses, the official turned to Boyd McBride's Kodak Instamatic, a Model 314, mass produced in such vast quantities that serial numbers were not even considered. After a lengthy argument about the requirement of listing serial numbers, Boyd pointed straightfaced at the front of the camera. "There it is," he announced triumphantly, "number 314." The official smiled happily, nodded, and painstakingly added this number to the form.

The procedure is as follows: all currency and travelers checks are listed on your form as you enter; each time you change money or cash a check, the bank notes the transaction on the reverse side; when you leave, the form is checked against the amount on your person. Be sure to declare everything—anything not listed can be

Barter in the desert.

confiscated when you exit.

Algeria, Congo (Kinshasha), and all three East African countries prohibit removal of their currency from the country. This situation gives rise to black markets, as explained earlier. So long as you are careful not to cash more than you can spend before leaving, however, it should not affect you otherwise. Make a practice of spending the balance of your local cash on fuel or groceries at the last town before the border. Just don't run out too soon and have to cash another check.

BARTER: STILL BIG IN THE DESERT:

Being a non-smoker, I failed to carry cigarettes—a sizable mistake. In the desert and Central Africa, natives almost invariably ask for a smoke—not so much for smoking as for a kind of primitive currency. If you want to make friends and influence the locals, carry a couple of cartons of L&M's, and give two or three to those who ask. After all, how often do you get a chance to be a hero for a nickel these days?

DEVALUATION:

Since my return from Africa, the dollar has been devalued twice—once in mid-1972, and again in early 1973. As a result, all prices, rates of exchange, and similar information in this book may have changed by as much as 20% to the worse. Prices and exchange rates vary from year to year in any event, and should be checked at the time of leaving or just after your arrival. As a further guide, you will find at the end of this book a chart of post-devaluation official exchange rates, which constitute the latest information available. Up-to-the-minute black market rates will have to await my next trip.

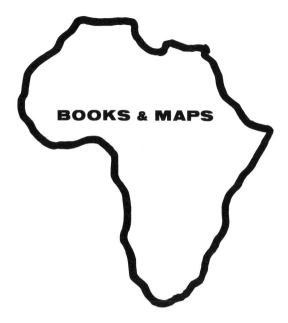

BOOKS & MAPS

I received some of the world's worst advice while preparing to jump off for Africa from southern Spain. I inquired about shots, visas, medicines, and border problems, and met with complete ignorance on all sides. Someone referred me to the U.S. Embassy in Madrid, which "would know all about that sort of thing."

Now, Madrid was one hell of a long way from where I was at the time. But, since there was no other source of information whatever, I went there and consulted the American Embassy staff. "Oh, yes," I was told, "we have information about African visas. Check that list on the wall over there." Sure enough, that list contained a complete enumeration of African nations requiring visas, together with addresses where one could inquire further—virtually all of which were located in New York City.

Not wishing to waste the trip entirely, I returned to my new-found mentor, and asked about shots and diseases. "Well," began the response, "the only disease that I know of that is any problem is cholera. You might get a cholera shot, but that should be all you'll need." It was much, much later that I learned about yellow fever, encephalitis, bilharzia, and a few other choice goodies. Needless to say, there was a definite lack of communication thereabouts.

In Malaga, Spain, I inquired at the VW agency, and was referred to "our expert on Africa." The expert turned out to be a ruddy-cheeked, clipped-speech Briton, who had "been all over down there."

"What about wide tires and wheels?" I asked. "Should I have a limited-slip differential? What do I need to keep from getting stuck?"

"No problem, no problem at all," he announced with an air of great experience. "Never get a Volkswagen stuck. Rear engine and all that, you know. You'll walk right on through." As you have already seen, that has got to be the worst piece of advice one human being could possibly give another.

When we started out across the Sahara, we had no idea whether we could make it in a two-wheel-drive vehicle, what the roads were like, or what kind of equipment we needed. When we got within a couple of hundred miles of a given area, we could begin to get some meaningful information about it. Before that, forget it.

It was just this lack of pertinent data that led me to write this book. I know what I would have given for a complete, how-to-do-it manual on crossing Africa. If this conglomeration of ideas and advice is one fifth as valuable to subsequent travelers, it will have served its purpose.

MICHELIN MAPS: THE GREATEST EVER:

The one sine qua non of African travel is the Michelin map. It contains a wealth of essential information: location of all petrol points; all water points in desert regions; degree of road maintenance or lack thereof; passability of roads during rainy seasons; time of rainy seasons; and location of hotels and mechanics. Such a goldmine of knowledge is absolutely indispensable.

The only fault I found was that the maps were slightly outdated. Road conditions were not always the same as depicted. In a continent as vast and changeable as Africa, this is to be expected. Supplement the maps with questions as you go, and you will be covered from all angles.

These maps are available in a series of three: Africa North and West, Number 153; Africa North and East, Number 154; and Africa Center and South, Number 155. Between them, they cover the entire continent, overlapping slightly. They can be bought in many European cities at a cost of $1 to $2 each—an excellent investment, to say the least. You may order by mail from: Michelin Tyre Co., Ltd., 81, Fulham Road, London, S.W. 3, England; or Pneu Michelin, Services de Tourisme, 97 Bd. Pereire, Paris, 17, France.

Another set of maps providing more detail, but over a much smaller area, are the Shell maps of East Africa. If you expect to spend a good deal of time there, they represent a sound expenditure at about a buck apiece. They also come in a set of three, covering Kenya, Uganda, and Tanzania, plus a fourth combining the other three, but at considerable loss of detail. These maps are a great help in pinpointing game preserves, national parks, and other points of interest. They can be had at almost any Shell service station in East Africa.

A BOOK FOR ALL SEASONS:

As far as books on how to travel in Africa are concerned, this is it. I know of no other book that even begins to prepare you for the full, transcontinental trip.

Language books are a great help. Your local bookstore can supply an English/French-French/English dictionary and a basic French grammar in paperback at nominal cost, for use in North, Central, and West Africa. A Berlitz or similar phrasebook is of little use. You won't have much occasion to say "Please take

Murchison Falls, Uganda, where the Nile River plunges through a gorge only 20 ft. wide, in a breathtaking burst of spray and foam.

these dresses to be cleaned" in Algeria. And you'll play hell looking up "I need a ring gear for the differential of a 1968 VW microbus" without a good dictionary.

Highly recommended is *Upcountry Swahili,* by F. H. Le Breton, published by R. W. Simpson & Co., Ltd., 70, Sheen Road, Richmond, Surrey, England, and available in book stores throughout East Africa for under $1. This pocket-sized manual will provide you with the basic vocabulary and simplified "upcountry" grammar necessary for most East African emergencies and social situations. Unless you wish to become a real Swahili scholar, stay away from the more complicated "coastal" Swahili textbooks. You probably won't be there long enough to learn it all; and natives away from the coastal regions don't use all that complex grammar anyway. You can get along without Swahili in any event, as most residents speak English. But you would miss the fun of communicating with the natives in their own language.

Basic handbooks on Afrikaans for use in South Africa are also obtainable in paperback. Here again, such a book is not essential, as almost all South Africans speak English. However, the Afrikaner segment of the population are very nationalistic. They are pleased to hear you essay a few words of their language, and often become irritated if you won't try.

An absolute must is an owner's manual and some sort of shop manual for the vehicle you are driving. If the official factory book is not available from the dealer, good substitutes can be found. An excellent example is *Volkswagen 1600 Technical Manual,* by Henry Elfrink, published by Henry Elfrink Automotive, P.O. Box 20367, Los Angeles, California 90006, at $5. Also good is *U.S. Army Technical Manual TM 9-8014,* covering all degrees of maintenance and repair of the Army Jeep. If copies are available, it can be purchased from Superintendent of Documents, U.S. Government Printing Office, Washington, D.C. 20402, for under $5. If not, try Arizona Ordnance Company, P.O. Box 20191, Phoenix, Arizona 85036. A whole slew of books on both American and foreign makes can be ordered by mail from: J.C. Whitney & Co., 1917 Archer Avenue, Chicago, Illinois 60616; or Warshawsky & Co., 1900 South State Street, Chicago, Illinois 60616. Or see your local dealer, parts house, or bookstore. A parts manual with exploded diagrams may seem like gilding the lily; but it sure takes care of the language problem, should you have to buy parts.

Medical books are another essential item. Something on the order of the *Modern Home Medical Advisor* is fine for treating routine injuries and ailments, but doesn't begin to meet Africa's peculiar problems. A layman's work on tropical diseases would help. If you can plough through its technical language, *The Merck Manual,* Merck, Sharp, and Dohme Research Laboratories, Professional Service Department, West Point, Pennsylvania 19486, at about $10, lists the symptoms, prognosis, and treatment for every known disease. You won't find this one in the bookstores—it is sold only to doctors. Perhaps you can con your doctor out of an outdated copy. After all, the symptoms of malaria can't change much between editions.

A valuable touring guide is Thornton Cox' *Travellers' Guide to East Africa,* published by Thornton Cox, 3 Colebrook Ct., Sloane Avenue, London, S.W. 3, England. It consists largely of excerpts from travel brochures about various East African tourist attractions, but is ideal to ensure that you don't miss anything. Cost: $1.75 anywhere in East Africa.

If you like to read for pleasure, a raft of paperbacks won't hurt. You'll have plenty of time to kill when camped in the desert at night or while waiting for a mechanic to install a new link pin. I won't presume to dictate your reading material, but suggest that you look along the way for books with an African flavor. You might as well soak up a little history and anthropology in dilute form, along with all that magnificent scenery. You can trade with other travelers as you go along— you'll have a completely refurbished library every month or so.

THE MAIL
PROBLEM

When setting out on this expedition, we never really expected to penetrate the Nigerian border. With this in mind, I had my mail sent to Cotonou, Dahomey, the jumping-off point for freightering around Nigeria. I notified all my correspondents before leaving Morocco, and left a forwarding address with American Express in Rabat, requesting transshipment of all mail to American Express in Cotonou.

When we gained entry to Cameroun, over a month later, I realized we would never reach Cotonou. I promptly telegrammed American Express there to forward all mail to the U.S. Embassy in Yaounde. As added insurance, I posted an airmail letter, duplicating the telegram. After another week, we reached Yaounde and the Embassy. No mail, of course.

A few days, another airmail letter, and an unsuccessful attempt to telex the Cotonou Embassy later, we decided to place a phone call. After all, Dahomey was only a few hundred miles away. The call was instituted through the U.S. Embassy switchboard, to alleviate the language problem, promptly at 8:30 A.M. the next day. As all long distance calls were routed through Paris, we settled back to wait. At 5:00 P.M., when the Embassy closed, we grew tired of waiting and canceled the call.

The Embassy ultimately got a telegram through to its alter ego in Cotonou, which called American Express and wired back, "No mail." I left a third forwarding address of Bangui, R.C.A.

In Bangui, two months after leaving Morocco, I finally received one water stained, tattered, and virtually illegible letter, out of a dozen or so that I know were sent. Not a very good average, all things considered.

At Ngorongora crater this lovely lady insisted upon taking the author's picture . . .

Residents of the various French-speaking countries in North, Central, and West Africa concede readily that the mails are a risky venture. While letters arrive quite reliably, the odds of receiving a package (which might contain something worth stealing) are estimated at about 50-50. Avoid sending or receiving anything of value when in these countries. In East and South Africa, the mails are far more reliable.

WHAT TO DO WITH COLOR FILM:

The processing of film rapidly degenerates into a mail problem, as all color film must be posted to London, Paris, or the U.S. for processing. And it must be mailed promptly, as high temperatures or humidity changes can harm the latent images on exposed film. African photography shops and film processing plants are not equipped to handle color film; in most instances, their handling of black and white leaves a great deal to be desired.

I circumvented this problem by sticking to black and white, having the negatives developed locally, and making my own prints back in the U.S. Since I made over 700 exposures, this resulted in a considerable savings in cost. Captain Deb went me one better. She took along a few cans of chemicals, a light tight changing bag, and a small tank for developing negatives. She not only reduced her costs more than I, but avoided all that rough handling and machine developing that is so hard on negatives.

90

... with surprising results. This is one of my better portraits.

If you are really hung on color, take with you a supply of those yellow Kodak film mailers. You can then mail your film direct to Kodak in New York, with instructions for them to return it to your stateside address. As exposed film is of little value, the risk of theft is minimized by using the yellow mailer. In a plain package, your film might get stolen despite its lack of value. Send home one roll at a time, each in its own package, so that you won't lose several rolls in one swell foop. You will find that this is an expensive process by airmail, but would take several weeks by surface vessel. That is part of the price for taking color pictures in Africa.

The only alternative is to trust to local photography shops to package the film, send it to London or Paris, and return it to them or you without loss. Risky, at best.

FORWARDING: THINK AHEAD:

Whenever possible, I had my mail forwarded to a city about one month ahead. Before leaving, I reduced my correspondents to about two, so that I would have fewer persons to notify of an address change. Anyone else wishing to contact me could do so by writing to my home address; the post office delivered all such mail to my next-door neighbor, who was one of the two; the neighbor would forward anything important, save routine mail for my return, and receive and hold packages from me in Africa.

A few days before leaving, say, Nairobi, I would write both my correspondents and leave word at the U.S. Embassy that all my mail should be forwarded c/o U.S Embassy, Cape Town, where I might reasonably expect to be four to six weeks later. By this method, I didn't outrun my mail so that it followed me from city to city, nor did I go without news from home for more than about a month.

Many of my fellow travelers cut it much closer, by requesting that all mail be sent to the next city down the line, but not after a specified date. They got their news faster, but may have lost a letter or two more. Your choice depends on how big a hurry your mail is in, and how critical is its possible loss. I left a forwarding address behind each time I left a city where I had received mail. On the entire trip, I received exactly two letters that had been correctly forwarded. The odds just aren't with you.

THE U.S. EMBASSY: YOUR BEST BET:

There are three places where you can receive mail in a strange city: General Delivery, called "Poste Restante" in French countries; c/o American Express; or c/o Visitors' Mail, U.S. Embassy.

None of the three charges for receiving and holding mail. If you have letters forwarded from one city to the next, American Express charges $2 per move, the Embassy nothing. Post offices vary; some might impose a slight fee.

Requirements to entitle you to such service? Post office, none; Embassy, a valid U.S. passport; American Express may or may not demand to see your travelers checks.

Every concentration of people large enough to be called a city has a post office and general delivery. Embassies are located in the capital city of each country, with perhaps a consulate in other large cities, if any. American Express offices exist in at least the most populous city in each country, and sometimes in others. A list of all such offices in the world can be had free at most American Express offices.

I have never really trusted African general delivery, although, if you have to rely on the post office to get the mail there, there's really no reason why you can't trust them to hold it for you for a while. Postal clerks in the more primitive areas are probably unaccustomed to American names, reading English, and dealing with tourists.

American Express mail clerks may or may not be a slight improvement. Most such offices are actually operated and staffed by a travel agency, which assumes the responsibility of taking care of American Express customers and handling their mail in exchange for the travel business it brings in. Handling your mail is not their primary concern, and is usually delegated to a secretary or clerk on a part-time basis.

Most reliable, in my opinion, are the American Embassies, which cannot afford to hire people who are not reasonably well educated and able to handle American tourists. I found the various Embassies to be far more efficient, and quite helpful about any problems you may have generally.

THEFT PREVENTION

As in any other sizable continent spanning many nations, the risk of theft in Africa defies application of any hard and fast rules.

In Malindi, Kenya, we met three members of Encounter Overland, a package tour. Groups such as this and another called Minitrek take vanfuls of tourists on motorized trips of varying length through the desert and into East Africa. Both are headquartered in London.

Aside from a certain degree of boredom and some striking personality clashes, we were told, one of their primary problems was theft. The group had been burgled six or seven times on the way south, to the extent that many had little or nothing left in the way of clothing or photographic equipment. On one occasion, according to our informants, the expedition's suitcases were all lashed down together inside the mess tent, and were rifled nonetheless while a round dozen people inside the tent ate dinner.

At the other extreme was my own experience. After being burgled once in Barcelona, I installed a bevy of locks and alarms. Thereafter, I was never once robbed or broken into throughout the whole of Africa.

TROUBLE AREAS:

The risk varies considerably from place to place. In Morocco, thievery is endemic. My experiences in the desert (see Chapters Two and Six) would indicate that no one is more honest than the true desert dweller. My Encounter Overland friends would obviously disagree.

In East Africa, public sentiment against thievery is overwhelming. While in Fort Portal, we saw a group of young lads tormenting another boy. They were jerking him roughly along by a rope around the neck. His hands were tied before him; blood streamed down his face from a cut over one eye; he was sobbing and cringing. As he passed us, one of his tormentors delivered a vicious kick to the small of his back.

Uncertain as to whether I should interfere, I asked a black passerby about the frightening scene being played out before us. "Oh, it is alright," he informed me cheerfully. "They have just caught a thief."

"What are they going to do with him?" I inquired, not quite satisfied.

"They are taking him to the police station. Once he gets there, he will be alright."

"A little rough, aren't they?"

"Oh, well, they used to kill them."

In a society that feels this strongly, you would expect the incidence of larceny to be almost nonexistent. And we were never bothered by it. Yet, comparatively well-to-do residents of the area had all been burgled several times. They had bars on their windows and askaris standing guard all night.

Few people starve in East Africa, as food grows so plentifully; but some suffer from malnutrition, and the great bulk of the populace live in poverty. The native in the bush who has naught but his straw hut, a few goats, and a half acre of manioc, surrounded by his fellows, is in most instances quite content. But the lure of the city is strong. More and more young men leave the family shamba each year, to live in Kampala or Nairobi. There, no job or place in society awaits them. Unemployed and unskilled, they live in vast, squalid slums. When they become sufficiently hungry and sufficiently desperate, here and there one may take to stealing.

South Africa presents a slightly different problem. She has undergone what can only be called "Americanization." Durban is much like Fort Lauderdale, Johannesburg like Chicago. There is one difference: the poorer class (in this case, the blacks) are not allowed in the white man's cities at night without an identification book showing that they reside at the site of their job there. As a result, the cities have no slums. Nevertheless, they do have theft. One of the major dangers in South African cities is the same as in New York or Chicago: that of being mugged.

In a situation so extremely variable, the only sensible approach is to exercise care at all times. Don't be paranoid—the great bulk of the people you meet will be honest, helpful, and trustworthy. But do be careful—all the time.

Particular trouble areas are all of Morocco, all big cities, and seaports. It is the citified native who has learned to steal as an offshoot of his civilization. The rural native living in the bush would never consider such a thing.

LOCKS, PAD- AND OTHERWISE:

There is, of course, no 100% protection against theft. No matter what precautions you may take, a determined professional thief will get into your vehicle, via a smashed window, by popping out your windshield, or by driving the cylinder through the door lock.

An example of this principle in action was the Australian I met in Bangui, driving a home-built camper. In a determined effort to thwart thieves, he had welded a sturdy, steel lock box to the floor of the van, and fitted it with a strong lock. He returned home late one night, to discover the box broken open and his cash and documents gone.

Another acquaintance, a young Canadian, slept out in the open air one night, in the nearest place of safety—the front lawn of a mission in Victoria, Cameroun. To safeguard his belongings, he tied his backpack to one leg. He awoke late in the night to find three thugs rifling his pack, which was still attached to his leg.

Your best approach is to take all possible precautions. They will discourage most casual burglars, and may make the professional decide to go find an easier target. Then quit worrying and enjoy yourself, as the matter is now out of your hands anyway. Some sensible measures follow.

Be sure all doors and openings into your vehicle lock securely—side and rear doors, pop-tops and windows, as well as the front doors. If necessary, buy and install extra automobile door locks or cabinet locks. Don't forget locking handles for trunk lid and engine compartment.

These and most other locks discussed here are available at your local parts house or hardware store, or by mail from: Warshawsky & Co., 1900 South State Street, Chicago, Illinois 60616; or J.C. Whitney & Co., 1917 Archer Avenue, Chicago, Illinois 60616. Buy as many of your locks as possible in a set with matching keys or combinations, so that you will be bothered with the fewest possible keys to carry and numbers to remember. Select combination locks with easy-to-remember numbers, such as 123, 995, etc.

You might install cabinet locks or padlocks on all interior cabinets, closets, and stowage spaces. Once inside, few thieves will be stopped cold by them. But they do have the advantage of putting the maximum number of obstacles in the way. Another line of thought is that once a burglar has gone that far, he will break up your cabinetry to get past the locks. Why not just leave them open for him?

All valuable equipment mounted outside the vehicle should also be locked. Lug nuts that cannot be removed without a key will secure the tires and wheels to your car. Bicycle locks, in the form of a loop of plastic-covered steel cable fastened by a small combination cylinder, will safeguard your spare tires, gas cans, etc. The better, steel petrol cans can be locked closed with a small padlock, in addition to being cabled to the car. Fuel is precious in the desert; don't risk it. For the same reason, purchase a locking gas cap to protect the fuel in your tank. Petrol cans, suitcases, and other items in your luggage rack can be secured to the rack by a length of steel chain with both ends padlocked together. Case hardened steel costs little more, and is far less easily cut through by burglars. Slide a long piece of garden hose over the chain, to prevent rattling and scratching.

Windows should also be safeguarded. Easiest access to your car is by jimmying the front vent window open about ⅛ inch, and inserting a bent piece of coat hanger, which is used to roll down the side window. The thief then simply reaches in the open window and opens the door. The first line of defense to this approach is a pair of small, aluminum-and-stainless clips, which secure the vent window to its frame so

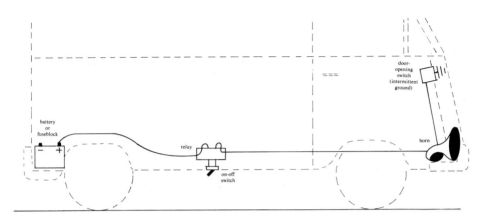

Auto alarm diagram

that it can't be jimmied outward. In addition, side window handles can be secured to the nearest stationary object, to prevent their being unwound, with short pieces of steel cable and small padlocks. More simply, inside door and window handles can be removed when parked in a high-risk location, and are easily replaced later.

ALARMS, SIRENS, AND A REAL SHOCKER:

Your last line of defense, should all of the above fail, is a burglar alarm. Any of several commercially manufactured models can be purchased from Warshawsky or Whitney, or from any auto accessory shop.

Some types operate via two small clips, that close in the side doors and are connected by wires to a battery-powered siren resting on the front seat. When a door is opened, the clip springs open, completing an electrical circuit that sounds the siren until its battery runs down. A trifle clumsy, but it works.

Others operate through a mercury switch that activates an alarm if moved or jostled, by a door opening and closing, for instance. Very effective, but a bit inconvenient if another car bumps yours while parking.

The most common type sounds your horn if a door is opened, by use of the switches that turn on your interior lights when you open the door, or with additional switches of the same design. It can utilize extra switches placed under the engine compartment lid and trunk lid. A disadvantage of this design is that it is easily turned off by the simple expedient of closing the open door.

A fourth type electronically senses any change in current from your battery, such as when the ignition starts, your dome light turns on, etc. Works fine if you have interior lights that go on as doors open.

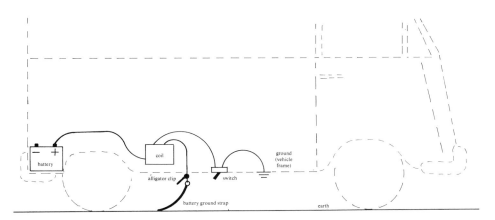

Auto shock diagram

A few facts to consider about the various types: Those operating through door switches are effective only if entry is made through a door; if through a window, they're not much use. Most professionals know enough to disconnect your horn leads before breaking in, thereby nullifying any device that utilizes your horn. This type does the job only with its own horn or siren, mounted in an inaccessible place. Models that sound until their batteries run down or they are turned off with a key are best. Battery replacement may be a problem with self-contained, battery-powered models.

Warshawsky lists eight different alarms, varying in price from $4.50 to $24.89. I built my own in Spain at a cost of under $4. With access to some junkyard parts, you can make one for almost nothing. See diagram above left.

Be sure to attach the hot wire to a power source that has juice when the ignition is off. The on-off switch should be mounted outside the car, so that you can turn it on after you have exited. A switch that operates only with a key is best. Otherwise, mount it inside your locked trunk or engine compartment. If you do not have lights that go on as the door opens, the switches for that purpose are easily added. If you already have them, try splicing into the wire leading to any one. They are usually interconnected, so that wiring your alarm to the other switches should be unnecessary.

A really different device is one that delivers an unpleasant, but relatively harmless shock to anyone who touches the car. It is easily constructed from a Model T coil, an on-off switch, some wire-centered, spark plug wire, an alligator clip, and an old battery ground strap. See diagram above right.

This design will not function with any other than a Model T coil, or other vibrator type coil. One can be purchased from J.C. Whitney or Warshawsky, for $7.95. Spark plug wire with a wire center is far preferable to the type with graphite core. Connect the hot wire to the third cell of your 12-volt battery, or install a 6-volt resistor between battery and coil. A rubber grommet around the hot wire where it passes through the frame is essential to avoid short-circuiting the system. All electrical connections should be soldered. Use a rubber covered handle for the switch, or dip it in epoxy or plastic, to avoid being shocked when turning the unit on or off. When leaving the car, attach the alligator clip to the exposed end of the hot wire, turn the switch on, and slop about a pint of water over the ground strap, to ensure a solid contact with the pavement. When returning, turn the switch off carefully before touching any other part of the car. Touching the hot wire or ground strap directly while switch is on can result in a nasty jolt.

A warning sign in your window is recommended. You could play hell explaining your behavior to a Nairobi traffic cop who tried to put a parking ticket under your windshield, or to the little old lady who put her hand on your fender to steady herself as she walked by. Don't forget a second sign in French for North, West, and Central Africa.

PARKING IS HALF THE BATTLE:
Whenever possible, park in a guarded lot or patrolled area when in cities. In some Moroccan cities, such as Rabat, a guard is assigned to each stretch of city street. Tip him a small amount as you leave; he's well worth it. Where there are no guards, lots of people and gobs of light are your best protection. We often parked in an open filling station or in front of the local police station—with permission, of course. With a little imagination, you'll find a spot that would be uncomfortable for burglars.

Most important, don't leave any loose articles in view. Stow everything out of sight before leaving the car. Objects of any kind lying about are an outright invitation to come on in and see what else is there.

INSURANCE:
As is mentioned in Chapter Ten, the only real protection against theft of the vehicle itself is comprehensive insurance good throughout the African continent. If your car is valuable, you should consider buying it.

As far as the contents are concerned, you get a second chance. Check your homeowner's policy—it may well cover theft or mysterious disappearance of articles normally kept in your home, no matter where in the world the loss occurs. Since your cameras, clothing, and camping equipment can honestly be said to be normally housed at home, you may already have coverage. Just be sure there is no exclusion denying liability if the loss is from an uninsured vehicle owned by the insured.

If you have no such homeowner's coverage, ask your insurance agent about a personal property "floater" covering such losses. It can probably be purchased separately, at moderate cost.

If you carry nothing of value with you, you may well prefer to take your chances.

Whether you are covered or not, don't relax your precautions. Loss of your documents, clothing, or camping equipment can play hob with a trip in which you have invested a great deal of time, effort, and money. Of course, the fewer valuables you carry, the less you will worry.

HANG ONTO THAT PASSPORT:

A black market in stolen and forged documents exists throughout most of the world. A U.S. passport is worth up to $250 or more. It is easy for the thief to carry away, conceal, and dispose of later.

Loss of your essential documents could stop you cold for several weeks. Imagine being stuck in a desert town such as Agadez, and trying to replace your passport through the American Embassy in Algiers, over 1,500 miles away; your auto registration and carnet from Germany or the U.S.; your shot card via the nearest hospital or clinic that can fill your arm with needles—wherever that might be; and travelers checks through an American Express office—ditto. And all before you can cross the next border.

I divided my documents into two batches. One, containing replaceable papers of no immediate value, I kept hidden in an inaccessible hiding place inside the van. Owners of a factory VW camper will find the spice rack on the side of the icebox ideal for this purpose. Almost any thief will break in through a front door. The hinged portion of the fold-down table covers the spice rack, and cannot be raised so long as the side door remains locked from the outside. In this configuration, the rack is both inconspicuous and difficult to break into. Many vehicles have similar cubbyholes. Check under interior floorboards, inside doors, and between interior and exterior body panels. An ounce of deception is worth any number of locks. If you can find a way to lock it in addition, so much the better. Photographic lenses and other small valuables can be hidden here along with your less valuable documents.

My really important papers were kept on my person at all times. Cash, travelers checks, passport, health certificate, vehicle title and registration, insurance certificate, and carnet all fall within this classification. The carnet, however, is so bulky that you will probably decide to hide it inside the car. You should leave with it some of your cash and travelers checks. If your wallet should be lost or stolen, you will need money to tide you over until you replace everything. Keep in your car a detailed list of all documents on your person, and vice versa, including serial numbers and replacement addresses. If either gets stolen, you will have a starting point for replacement.

Do not under any circumstances tote your valuables in a pocket. They would be stolen during your first week in Morocco, where pickpockets abound, or inevitably lost at some time during the ensuing six months. Carry them under your clothing in a money belt or wallet, where they won't be lost or "picked."

There are three types of wallet in common use. One is the conventional money belt, worn around the waist, consisting of a wide, canvas belt, with built-in pockets and button-down flaps. It does the job, but is a trifle uncomfortable.

A second design is a simple pouch worn on a cord about the neck. This is also adequate, but can tire the neck muscles, and bounces against the chest when its wearer is running. I manufactured one of these from a linen handkerchief and a piece of nylon cord.

Possibly the best of the three is a similar pouch, with a longer cord or strap going over one shoulder, so that the wallet rests under the other arm. If you want to get really fancy, add a second strap crossing the chest horizontally to hold it snugly in place.

STRICTLY SMALL CHANGE:

An Arab in Tangier treated us to a dazzling display of consummate thievery. He approached us on the street, and asked if we could change some foreign coins that someone had passed off on him. He held out a U.S. quarter and a British fifty-new-pence piece, offering to accept "anything, anything at all for them."

Tempted, perhaps, by this unbeatable rate of exchange, Boyd McBride fished a handful of Spanish pesetas and Moroccan dirham from his pocket. To these, our Arab added his two coins, so that Boyd stood there staring at four different currencies, some of which did not even belong to him, while exchange rates caromed off one another inside his skull.

With a quick, pointing motion, the Arab tapped a coin in Boyd's hand, moved it with a fingertip, then tapped another, all the while keeping up a rapid stream of chatter, discussing the possible combinations of coins that would pay for his two. Boyd instinctively recoiled, pulling his hand protectively closer to his body. Our friend apologized profusely, patted him on the arm, then tapped his palm with an extended forefinger once, twice more.

Now, I knew Boyd was losing some money; but I couldn't quite see how. I was curious, and decided to risk a handful of change to get a better look. Within a minute, we had gone through the exact same process with my money. Then our prestidigitating friend decided that he had wanted French francs all along, retrieved his two coins from my outstretched palm, and disappeared.

Boyd and I concluded we had been clipped for about $1.75 between the two of us. The Arab had concentrated on getting about three large coins from each of us, ignoring the smaller pieces. I had stood there watching him do it several times over, knew what was happening, and yet could not see how he managed it.

I promptly bought a small, cleverly folding, Moroccan change purse to hold my coins. I doubt, however, that you'll encounter this sort of problem often enough to worry about it.

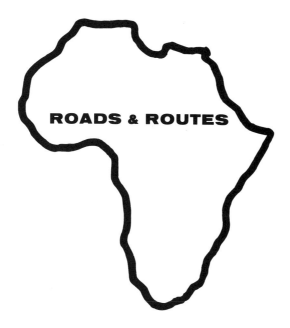

ROADS & ROUTES

We made Bangassou after four days (and fourteen flat tires) on 40 m.p.h. washboard roads. It was here that we were to catch the ferry across the Ubangi and into the Congo. There was only one hitch—the ferry was out of commission.

As usual, rumors abounded. We could not get across. We could cross on a native raft laid on top of five pirogues for $20. For $50. We could cross for free, if we could supply two twelve-volt batteries to start the ferry engine. Time alone would tell.

Rumor number two turned out to be fairly accurate. After a minimum of haggling, several natives at the landing agreed to take us across for $20 per vehicle. We watched sceptically as ten of the local boys assembled five dugout canoes, laid two stout two-by-twelves across them, and tied the entire assembly together with a single, seemingly endless rope. Rube Goldberg would have burst with pride on viewing the result. I drove gingerly onto the two planks.

The ten entrepreneurs then paddled us smoothly a good half mile across the Ubangi, keeping time to a polyrhythmic African chant all the while. Our freeboard was as much as five inches in places. Emulating George Washington, I stood up in the boat to pose for pictures. All in all, it was quite an experience.

African roads are full of little surprises—some good, some godawful. I will try, in this chapter, to prepare you for them, area by area.

NORTH AFRICA:

Morocco is a land of smooth, paved roads and large numbers of donkey carts. By sticking to the main thoroughfares indicated on your Michelin map, you should be able to go almost anywhere at speeds above 50 m.p.h. The primary speed inhibitor here is all that foot and donkey-cart traffic. Most carts are built on automobile rear axles, with empty differential housings hanging down beneath, as a sort of ambulatory phallic symbol. There are some rough stretches on the secondary roads, that may slow you down, but not enough to stop your forward progress or make things really difficult.

Northern Algeria is smooth as the proverbial baby's bottom. Beautiful, 70 m.p.h., paved highways reach as far south as Adrar. From Adrar south, things get a mite rough. See the next section for this one.

I have no personal experience of Libya or Egypt, and so will not comment on them here, except to note that my trusty Michelin map indicates one primary road along the Mediterranean coast of Libya, and that Egypt will not let you drive on her roads in any event.

TRANS-SAHARA:

There are four routes through, around, and over the vast desert region that blankets the northern third of the African continent. All involve a modicum of difficulty. One is closed to vehicular traffic. Any of the remaining three present a combination of exciting challenge and splendid scenery that will make up the greatest traveling experience of your life. Don't miss it if you have a choice.

Crossing the Ubangi . . . one at a time.

First is the western route, through Mauretania and possibly Spanish Sahara. From Tindouf, Morocco, to Richard Toll, Senegal, is 1,222 miles—all desert track. We were advised to avoid this route, as Spanish Sahara would deny us entry, and because the many miles of deep, loose sand were entirely too rough. If you can do the northern part of the trek through Spanish Sahara, you will have only 864 miles of sand track. Doesn't sound quite so bad; but, then again, I haven't seen it. Offhand, I'd recommend avoiding this one.

The eastern route extends across the top of Libya to the Egyptian border at Soloum—and then stops cold. At the time of my trip, Egypt would admit tourists, but would not let them drive anywhere. Apparently, they fear that you will run about photographing military installations, then blabber to the Israelis. The way things have been going over there, I wouldn't anticipate an especially early end to this restriction. To complicate things even further, the Sudan was engaged in a civil war while we were in Africa. If the situation ever stabilizes, the trip along the Red Sea might well prove to be the easiest, and that up the Nile by far the most interesting. For the time being, forget it.

There are two more or less parallel tracks through the center of the Sahara, both of which are rough, but passable. The harder of the two is the Gao-Timbuktu route, running from Adrar south through Reggane and Tessalit to Gao, then on to Niamey, in Niger. The 863 miles of sand track include a goodly amount of soft sand. The map indicates 570 miles without petrol; we were told over 800. If the gas point at Tessalit were out, that would make the total 863. Better check thoroughly before setting out. We drove the northernmost 86 miles of this track, and found it to be among the worst we encountered. You will find it described in Chapter One. If the rest is anything like that first stretch, you'd better take the Hoggar track.

Last and best is the Hoggar track, running South from El Golea through In Salah, Tamanrasset, Tegguiddan-Tessoum, and Agadez, then on to Zinder, in Niger. The northern stretch, from El Golea to In Salah, is reputed to be extremely rocky and hard on tires. If you are lacking four-wheel drive, take it. It can't be much worse than all that soft sand and washboard we took from Adrar to Reggane to In Salah. From In Salah to Agadez is rock, hardpan, and washboard, a rough but drivable, 40 m.p.h. road, interspersed with plenty of soft sand and unmarked track near the Niger border. Between Agadez and Zinder was the worst loose sand we had yet been through. If you can, head southwest from Agadez to Birni-Nkonni—you'll find the going easier. Longest stretch without gas: a manageable 557 miles.

Roads in Niger are a mixture of loose, but smooth dirt, sand, and washboard. Fine in the dry, but could be difficult during the rainy season.

WEST AFRICA:

In West and Central Africa, you will begin to notice a peculiar fact. Each time you pass through a border station to exit from a country, the road degenerates into a wretched path, hardly suitable for cattle, until you reach the border station for entering the adjacent country. Money for road maintenance is apparently so precious that neither nation will accept the responsibility of improving and maintaining the piece of road between border posts.

Nigeria is an extremely crowded nation, cramming over 56 million residents into an area twice the size of California. Roads are, by African standards, excellent. Most are smooth, two-lane asphalt, with a four-lane expressway for a few miles. A jarring note is the heavy traffic. Trucks and homemade busses full to overflowing with seething masses of humanity race along at unrealistic speeds. Accidents can be disastrous. We narrowly missed one in which a lorry overturned, killing ten hitchhiking natives who had been riding up top. Take it easy and keep your eyes open. It beats digging out of the sand every two or three miles.

Cameroun, which I suspect is more typical of West African nations, has hard, washboarded, rock roads, with occasional potholes, good for a speed of about 45. No real problem here.

It is in West and Central Africa that the driving seems most primitive. Now that you are past the Sahara, goats and chickens, two of the world's least enlightened animals, will dash out at you without warning, as if hellbent on committing suicide. Avoid them if you can, of course, but not at the risk of causing an accident. Far better to kill a chicken accidentally, than to run another car off the road or to injure a pedestrian or your passengers, far from the closest doctor.

If you do hit an animal, *keep going*. We were told repeatedly not to stop for this purpose. You would quickly become involved in a brouhaha of gargantuan proportions: a maddened owner demanding $50 for his prize chicken, in Hausa; you helplessly pleading innocence in English; and the entire village surrounding you, all gesticulating and talking at once. Things could even get a little nasty.

Now, I know you are going to rebel at this next piece of advice; but here it is anyway. If you should hit a native pedestrian, don't stop. Step on the accelerator and head straight for the nearest police station. Many African tribes hold a man responsible for the net results of his actions, whether they were intended or not. An African who accidentally kills his brother while hunting may well be considered a murderer. To make things even worse, the bush African regards the automobile as a kind of magic. He doesn't realize that it is composed of mechanical devices that are all too fallible and subject to human error. He believes that it goes where you point it; if you hit someone, it is because you pointed it at him. Result: if you should accidentally kill a villager and stop to help, you may well be executed on the spot as a fair and just retribution for your crime. No matter how much it may go against the grain, *keep going* . . . to the nearest police station.

CENTRAL AFRICA:

Roads in the Republic of Central Africa are much like those in Cameroun: hard rock, potholed, washboarded, and good for about 40 m.p.h.

Congo (Kinshasha) is something else again. The French missionary at Mungbere had told us (or so I thought) to take the shortcut between Mambasa and Beni. We began on a narrow, rock road that became progressively narrower and rougher, until it deteriorated into a ribbon of rock hardly wider than the van, surrounded by dense jungle on either side. At first, we kept saying, "It'll get better in a mile or two, and we can get going again." It got worse. A deep, narrow gully, a relic of last year's rainy season, gradually developed, meandering aimlessly along its length. A

Children—from Morocco . . .

wheel in that gully would put us out of commission for quite awhile; and the road was too narrow to drive alongside it. I must have done twenty miles, precariously straddling that ditch and duplicating its tortuous path, at about 5 m.p.h. Add a few rocks, some bumps and holes, and you've got the picture.

"It'll get better in a mile or two" changed to, "If only we'd come to a spot wide enough to turn around in," and finally, "Jesus, we can't go back through all that." The road degenerated steadily. We were jouncing along painfully at under 5 m.p.h., stripped to a pair of shorts apiece in the sticky heat, when a swarm of tse tse flies appeared from absolutely nowhere and blanketed our bodies. I saw my arms turn black with insects, and felt the stinging fire of bites all over my body. I remember shouting something to the effect of "get 'em off me! Get 'em off me!" and taking a couple of swipes at my left arm with my right hand before we hit the boulder. We came to an agonizing, crunching stop, clutch jammed, engine racing. God knew what else was damaged.

We rolled up the windows and sprayed the VW with Raid—to the choking point. It did the job. I picked dead tse tse flies out of the oddest nooks and crannies for months afterward. When they disappeared (as suddenly as they had arrived), we surveyed the damage. We had dented the front bumper, removed the stabilizer bar from the car in toto, bent one steering arm in a ludicrous arc, smashed the heating

to Central Africa.

tunnel, bent the accelerator cable and clutch cable housing tubes, torn loose an axle boot, and bent a rear wheel so that it rubbed against a brake line on each revolution. We were about forty miles from the nearest town.

We somehow got under way again, and limped on toward Beni. But the Congo wasn't through with us yet. It began to rain. The erstwhile rock road turned into a slippery layer of clay. Crippled as we were, we got stuck, pushed it out, and got stuck again. We ultimately covered the 86 miles from Mambasa to Beni in eleven hours. That had to be the worst day of the trip.

In Beni, our luck changed. With one eye on the Ugandan border a scant few miles away, we bought a minimum of petrol and a loaf of fresh bread. I had left 150 Congolese mukudu and some $50 travelers checks. Unbelievably, we found a complete French machine shop, where we bent everything back to some semblance of normality. The bill: 150K. We were practically in Uganda.

All Congolese roads are not quite so horrible; but they are bad. Rock, gravel, and clay, most become a sea of slop during the rainy season. A fair gravel road runs East from Kisangani; it is one of two or three good roads in the country. Suggestion: map out the shortest possible route through the Congo. (We saved 417 miles of Congo driving by heading East in R.C.A. to cross at Bangassou, and passing up the conventional ferry at Bangui.) Go before the rainy season begins. And ask about

A captivating view of Lion's Head, towering over a residential area of Cape Town, South Africa.

each road as you go. Ask two or three people about each road as you go.

After seeing countless goats throughout West and Central Africa, you will be surprised to find none in the Congo. We were at a loss to explain this peculiar phenomenon, until we asked a missionary. "Oh, the goats were all eaten during the revolution," she told us. "Both armies took all the goats they could find for food. Now, there simply aren't any more." Judging by their record in other areas, however, I feel sure that they will somehow manage to repropagate themselves.

EAST AFRICA:

East African roads, by comparison, are almost sensuously comfortable. Most main arteries are smooth, two-lane asphalt, good for over 60 m.p.h. Some are earth and rock, called "murram", only slightly rough when dry, a slippery mess, but passable, in the rainy season. As long as it's not raining, you'll be OK. Again, ask as you go. Once you reach this point, your days of getting stuck are about over.

There is one really bad stretch in Tanzania, running from Dar Es Salaam southwestward to Zambia, that is aptly titled the "Hell Run". Tanzania is one of the few African nations that has reached a rapprochement with Red China. The Hell Run is cluttered with huge, Chinese lorries, driven by neat, cleanly groomed Chinese, all of a military age and bearing. The trucks carry mining equipment from the port at Dar to the copper mines of Zambia, and loads of iron ore back to Dar.

These trucks have not only pounded the road into a mass of dusty potholes, but throw up huge dust clouds in their wake, so that it is virtually impossible to see around two or three of them to pass. It is the only route from East to South Africa, and can be an unsettling experience.

We ran parallel to a new, paved highway under construction for much of the Run, and were even privileged to drive on it for short distances. By the time you get there, it may well be completed, reducing the Hell Run to something on the order of "Oh, Pshaw".

SOUTH AFRICA:

South Africa has fine, paved roads almost everywhere; Rhodesia and South West Africa feature well paved main routes, with some gravel and earth. There is even an expressway or two. In Rhodesia, you may find a leftover "strip road" here and there: two slim strips of asphalt, one for each wheel of your vehicle. If you meet another car, each relinquishes one strip until it is past. Quaint, but effective.

South Africa's roads have become so modernized that I had the typically American experience, while driving through the supposedly wild and primitive Kruger National Park, of being arrested for speeding—by radar.

Zambia, Malawi, and Mozambique have some paved roads, some good gravel, and some earth. Main thoroughfares are usually fairly good. The Zambia section of the Hell Run is a positive delight. But watch those earth roads in the rainy season. Mozambique in the rain can be a mess.

At the end of this book is a chart of all the roads I actually drove while in Africa. Things change in time, especially roads; but reference to this chart, your Michelin map, and the advice of locals and fellow wayfarers should keep you out of trouble.

THE SHORT TOUR:

This is the section you've all been waiting for: how to avoid all that mud, sand, and misery you've been reading about. It's not that bad, really; and it's the only thing that keeps parts of Africa primitive and exciting. If easy, paved highways were everywhere, the entire continent would look like Detroit within a few years. You will rapidly find that, in order to get away from other tourists, to see Africa in the raw, and to communicate with really unspoiled natives, you will have to get off the pavement and put up with some rough tracks.

At any rate, the short tour is simplicity itself. Stick to South and East Africa and parts in between. With the exception of the Hell Run, the rainy season, and a few secondary tracks, this area offers fair to excellent roads, an absence of intestinal diseases, drinkable water at every filling station, supermarkets, and a pub at the end of every day's haul. And the greatest tourist attractions of Africa are right there in Uganda, Kenya, and Tanzania.

If you have no desire for a difficult, months long journey, just travel by plane or ship to Cape Town, Durban, Mombasa, or Nairobi, and motor about to your heart's content. It's a piece of cake.

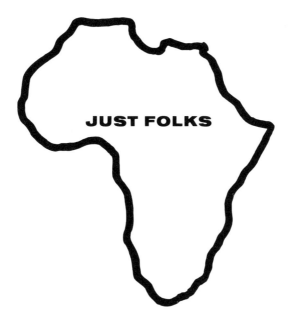

JUST FOLKS

The African continent is home for many diverse and fascinating peoples—from the wanderers of the northern desert to the proud Zulu of South Africa. On any lengthy journey, you will encounter many different tribes. It is helpful to have some idea of what to expect.

WANDERERS ALL:
Principal among North African population groups are the Bedouin. A semitic race, commonly referred to as Arabs, they are slim and tan in color. Those who have not settled in Morocco's towns and cities still follow the traditional ways of their people. They migrate from place to place in the desert, living in rude, goathide tents. We encountered Bedouin families living in some of the most inaccessible and uninviting places imaginable, surrounded by wastes of sand and little else, and surviving on who knows what.

The patriarch of one such family waved us down miles from any kind of town or waterhole. As he approached the car, we speculated on what he would try to bum from us. To the contrary, with great dignity, he proffered us a bowl of unappetizing and unclean milk—a lot more than one could expect under the circumstances. I regret to add that I did not have the guts to accept.

Another Bedouin whom we met at the Niger border at Assamaka was not quite so generous. He approached John Ibbotson, our own version of Good Sam, while John stood beside the camper eating dinner. He pointed at a cup of water; John gave him water. He then indicated a partial loaf of bread on the sideboard; John handed it to him silently. Riding his winning streak, the Arab pointed toward another hunk of

Tall and lithe, the Masai possess great dignity, even in youth.

bread on our table; again John complied. Waiting to see what would happen next, our British Samaritan stood motionless, a handful of dates in his left hand, an orange in the right. Without asking, the Bedouin reached out, took the dates, hesitated but a second, seized the orange, then stood waiting. John shrugged, palms up, in a universal gesture of emptiness. The Arab vanished instantly into the gathering darkness. Throughout the entire transaction, not a single word was spoken.

Both the Bedouin and another desert tribe, the Touareg, dress in long, loose robes and hoods. Touareg men, rather than their women, wear veils. Not only are such clothes necessary for warmth during the 40° desert nights, but they also provide a layer of insulating air between the skin and the sun's piercing rays. The Touareg, however, would seem to have some preternatural resistance to heat; some subgroups of their tribe wear only one shade or another of dark blue.

The Touareg boast a colorful history as dashing cavalrymen. If the blue man who traveled with us for half a day is any example, they have become an exceptionally friendly and peaceful people. Many make their way in the world raising camels, or driving camel trains from oasis to oasis, to exchange loads of desert salt for various items of food and clothing.

A third northern tribe, the Berbers, inhabit much of the area around the Atlas mountains. The ladies of the tribe wear chin tatoos, though you will seldom get a glimpse of one.

AFRICA PROPER:

From the northern border of Niger South, one is in what John Ibbotson describes as "Africa Proper", perhaps more widely known as Black Africa. It is in this area that the skin color of the predominant tribes shades from a dark tan into deep brown and black, and the faces begin to sport ceremonial scars.

The Hausa, a major tribe of traders, wander about engaging in commerce, throughout a huge area encompassing Niger and Nigeria. In fact, the Hausa tongue has become a sort of universal trade language far beyond the borders of their home country.

As we entered this area, we noticed several handsome, brown-skinned women walking about barebreasted, with no apparent sign of self-consciousness. Others of their tribe wore a sarong-like garment, composed solely of a few yards of brightly colored fabric, passing over the breasts and under the arms, and falling almost to the ground. A good number carried babies slung on their backs in a fold of this garment.

All of the barebreasted girls that we saw, even the young ones, sagged fantastically. We speculated at some length as to the possible causes for this phenomenon: dietary deficiencies, some obscure tribal practices, the total absence of brassieres. None made much sense. It was only after several weeks that it finally hit me. After she had one child, a girl spent the next year or two with anywhere from ten to twenty pounds of baby hanging in the dress on her back, and supported by nothing other than her bosom.

Another Central and West African tribe is the Fulani, whose members occupy much of the area around Cameroun. Traditionally herdsmen, many have long since adapted to city life. We were befriended by one such young man in Yaounde, who took us to his closet-sized room for a "shower", obtained by hauling three or four buckets of water up from a well and pouring them over oneself in a three-sided shack with a hole in the floor. Considering the length of time we had been without, it was heaven.

As we left his home, in the early evening, we heard the pulsating sound of polyrhythmic drums from a nearby house. Emmanuel, our friend of the shower, informed us that a neighborhood dance was in progress. We went closer to investigate, and were invited into a small room packed with people. An open space was cleared in the center, where two people danced to the beat of a native rhythm section: two hollowed logs, two waist-high tom toms, and two notched sticks rubbed with smaller sticks. Fantastic multiple rhythms were created by this crude assortment of instruments—far beyond the abilities of any "civilized" groups I have ever heard.

After a moment, one dancer returned to his seat; the other selected a partner from the audience. They moved sinuously together (or apart) for awhile before the selector sat down; the selectee then picked a substitute. This rotation of partners continued throughout the evening. The high point of the night's entertainment occurred when an unsuspecting black woman chose Rick Merry as her partner. Canadian teenager Rick let fly with the Frug, or the Watusi, or some such, to the delight of one and all.

Scattered throughout the tropical rain forests of Central Africa are the Pygmy, a diminutive people averaging about 4½ feet tall. While Pygmies have traditionally made their way in the world by hunting with poisoned arrows and woven nets, some now support themselves by posing for pictures and selling tourist items to travelers. Those near the Uganda-Congo border West of Fort Portal have been known to stone passing autos in outraged retaliation for their failure to stop and pay tribute. Those we met were far more primitive—and friendly.

GOD'S CHOSEN PEOPLE:

Two black tribes predominate in East Africa: the Kikuyu and the Masai.

The Kikuyu inhabit the Kenya uplands, fertile, rolling hills, stolen by the invading European for his vast plantations and ranches. They are quite dark, industrious, and adaptable to civilization. Today, many hold jobs as clerks, retail salespeople, and in similar occupations.

The Kikuyu revolted in the 1950's, fomenting the bloody Mau Mau rebellion. One of their leaders, Jomo Kenyatta, promptly took advantage of the revolution to assume leadership of the emerging nation, and today presides as chief of state of Kenya, most prosperous and stable of all black African countries.

The Masai are still more colorful. Still living the life of their predecessors since time immemorial, they have resisted civilization far more successfully than most African tribes.

Masai are tall and lithe, tinted a rich, chocolate brown, and bear themselves with a great dignity, approaching arrogance. Their traditional dress consists of a rusty brown cloak, a short iron broadsword, and a carefully plaited hairdo plastered with

clay the color of red ocher—the men, that is. The women shave their heads, and wear necklaces of red, white, and blue beads.

Their traditional way of life is that of the herdsman. They consider themselves "God's Chosen People", and firmly believe that the Almighty gave the cattle to the Masai, and to no one else. So ardent is this belief that Masai have been known to attack other Africans and seize their domestic animals as some sort of contraband. Naturally enough, this kind of behavior leads to strained relations with one's neighbors.

The Masai live almost entirely on cow's milk, mixed with blood artfully drawn from the neck of the animal, and spiced with just a touch of cattle urine and wood ashes. For the most part, they reject the white man's medicine, so that many are gradually dying off from syphillis. To complicate matters, they inhabit areas in southern Kenya and Northern Tanganyika, which are also needed by the vast, migrating game herds of Serengeti. Living off their cattle, they do not hunt; but the competition for space and grazing land unfortunately endangers either the Masai or the already threatened animals at every turn.

THE JEWS OF AFRICA:

Numerous throughout the eastern coastal areas of both East and South Africa are Indians. Having migrated from India generations, or even centuries ago, most are genuine Africans in every sense of the word. Unfortunately persona non grata in most countries, they are today's closest facsimile to the man without a country.

Indians in Africa suffer from many of the Jews' perennial problems: they are visibly different in both color and dress; they make good livings as merchants and moneychangers; they hoard their earnings, and send them outside the country for the saving; they will not deign to associate or intermarry with the indigenous population. In brief, the Indians insist upon remaining separate and aloof.

Visit the great nations of the world, and you will inevitably find man hating and fearing his fellow man, whom he regards as somehow inferior. The Irish Catholic, after decades of strife, still hates the northern Protestant. In our own country, the Irish, then the Jews, followed by Puerto Ricans, and always the Black, have come in for their share of hatred and abuse. In France, Blacks are treated equally; but the Algerians are discriminated against. Even in Israel, where of all places man should love and help his brother in the common fight against outside persecution, we find internal strife. The mideastern, or Sephardic Jew contends that his European counterpart has all the better jobs, the finer positions in society, and favoritism from the Government. The European Israelite, in rebuttal, claims that his eastern brother is uneducated, shiftless, and lazy, and makes no effort to improve himself or his country. Now, doesn't that all sound just a trifle familiar?

What is this ubiquitous force that drives man to discriminate against his fellow man? The scientific term is "xenophobia", from the Greek, meaning "fear of strangers". It appears to be an almost universal drive in humans and some other primates to band together with those of similar appearance, background, and belief, and to oppose all others as enemies.

Two Masai matrons.

The popular anthropological writer, Robert Ardrey, lays this trait to man's early development. Prehistoric man found himself forced into hunting or food-gathering bands of a size conducive to mobility, self defense, and feedability. And of course it had to repel all other groups, to retain a hunting territory sufficient to sustain it. Because of the severe competition for food, those with the strongest tendency to band together and force out intruders stood the best chance of survival. Thus have we evolved into a race of xenophobes.

Whatever the cause, the Black is the focus of South Africa's xenophobia, the Indian of East Africa's. I met a Kikuyu accountant in a Nairobi bar one night; and, as fellow drinkers do the world over, we fell to discussing the problems of the world we live in.

"The only thing I don't understand about you Americans," my newly acquired drinking buddy demanded with some asperity, "is why you treat your Blacks so badly!"

"I'm not sure I know," I replied. "And I'm not at all proud of it; but I think it's the same reason you Kenyans treat your Indians so badly." My friend wore a thoughtful expression for some minutes thereafter.

When Kenya obtained her independence in 1963, her Indians were given a choice of becoming citizens of Kenya or of the United Kingdom. The majority, fearing reprisals at the hands of the newly independent Kikuyu after generations of making money from them in shops and stores, opted for the British passport. The wily British, however, attached a condition allowing admittance to England herself only to those who entered before a specified date.

As a result, most East African Indians hold British passports, not good for entry into Britain, and are being gradually forced out of their businesses and homes by a Kenya government unsympathetic to those who have rejected its citizenship. They cannot "go home to India", as is so often bitterly suggested, as they have, for the most part, never lived there, and have no Indian passports.

What will ultimately happen to these enterprising and industrious people, only time can tell. Hundreds of thousands of Jews tried unsuccessfully to flee Europe in the late thirties; but few countries would have them. One would think that the great nations of the world—most especially Great Britain—would make some effort to find a home for the "Jews of Africa."

After the initial draft of this book had been submitted to my publisher, the government of Uganda expelled all its Asians, and confiscated their stores, homes and property. To its credit, Great Britain accepted large numbers of the refugees in London.

ABOUT APARTHEID:

The Indian in South Africa is not a whole lot better off. While it is the black man who receives the worst treatment there, the Indian, or any other "person of color" is also treated as less than a first class citizen.

Muhammed, a kindly Indian, befriended me in the Durban customs office, and took me for a rare, inside look at his mosque, as well as to his home. He summed up the situation as follows: "They only give us the crumbs here; but they are good crumbs; so we stay."

If the Indians get the crumbs, it is difficult to define what the Blacks get. All Blacks must live on a Bantustan, named after the huge group of African tribes homogeneously known as Bantu, and similar to an American Indian reservation. There, they may rent at modest cost a two-room house of the simplest sort, built in long row after row, all identical, with no variety whatever in color, shape, or placement. The street and development plans in some Bantustans are laid out to provide for easy control by the police or military in the event of insurrection.

A Black who has the money may build a finer house on a larger lot; but I never saw such a house during my stay. The only Bantu allowed to live outside the reservation are those who reside at their place of employment in a white area—mostly personal servants. Each Black must carry an identification book specifying his place and hours of work. If he is apprehended outside the Bantustan after curfew hours without a permit to live at his job site, he is subject to arrest and imprisonment. The book must be signed by his employer each week, so that he cannot use it after he has quit his job or been fired.

The Bantu are taxed; and many do not have the jobs or money with which to pay. As punishment, they are sentenced to short terms in jail. There, they can languish in durance vile, or work for a South African White for a blanket to sleep under, a few cigarettes, three squares, and about twenty cents a day.

All jobs are classified. Higher paying occupations to Whites; less enjoyable and renumerative ones to Blacks. In addition, a crazy quilt of laws and regulations effectively prevents a laborer from returning to his family home after accepting employment in the city. Thus, it can become a crime to sleep under the same roof as one's father or wife, under certain conditions of employment. While in Durban, I read a newspaper article about a black labor union insisting on pay raises to 16.40 Rand (about $23) per month total wages.

The Afrikaner has no trouble finding something to be said in support of the system. South Africa is one country in which the Europeans did not steal the land from the Africans. The early Dutch settlers arrived at about the same time as the Zulu, the Hottentot, and the Bushman, and so might well claim prior right to the land they settled.

It is the Afrikaner's perennial claim— and it appears to be quite true—that the Black in South Africa, on average, has a better life, economically speaking, than in any other African country. The two-room houses in the Bantustan rent for only $3 per month (the occupant's employer pays another $8). They are neat, clean, and a vast improvement over the squalid mud huts one sees throughout Central and East Africa. Nor is unemployment a major problem in South Africa, as it is amongst the teeming thousands in Nairobi's slums.

The Bantustans do include some beautiful country—mile after mile of rolling hills, and some black towns, too. All told, they constitute a considerable portion of the nation—not, of course, equal to the 70% which the Bantu comprise of the total population.

One must make a value judgment as to whether the economic improvement is worth the lack of personal freedom, the absence of opportunity for meaningful advancement, and the degradation of constant segregation. Separation of the races is

, Central African mud hut . . . versus . . .

rigidly enforced, not just in schools and government facilities, but in restaurants, hotels, and private homes. There are even separate mail windows in the post office, different counters in banks, and distinct bus lines: one white and one black. It is a crime for both Black and White if they should eat or drink at the same table, or sleep under the same roof.

The white man fears that enfranchising the Blacks, who outnumber him nine to one, will result in the loss of the modern cities, industrial plant, and other property that has been built with European know-how. There is some justice to this contention, as nationalization has occurred in most independent, black African countries. One cannot help but understand the desire of a man to keep and protect what he has devoted his life to building up. Of course, such an argument overlooks the fact that these things were also built with the labor of Bantu convicts, whose only crime was that they did not choose to have a European-style paying job.

Despite all this, I found European South Africans to be among the world's friendliest and most hospitable people. They are generally of two types: those of British origin, and the Afrikaners, descendants of the early Dutch settlers. The Afrikaners are stern, religious, in control of the Government, and are the moving force behind apartheid. The British are much like Englishmen everywhere. From both groups, I was treated with unbelievable hospitality—much like that in the American old West, before we became a race of city dwellers smothered in

... Bantustan housing project.

concrete. Complete strangers took me in off the street, to share their homes with me as if I were a member of the family. Of course, I had the advantage of being white.

Aside from a few, short conversations, I never had the opportunity to become friends with a black South African. Apartheid never really gave me the chance. They seem orderly and quiet, but sullen and hangdog at the same time. They do not look you in the eye and grin, as do the natives in most of Africa.

The Zulu are the oldest and largest South African tribe. They are tall and straight, descended from powerful armies of warriors, and still carry themselves with dignity. Many keep a walking stick handy, for all have been trained since infancy in stick fighting.

The Bushmen of South West Africa are a proud, silent group, who still live the traditional life of their ancestors. Few have condescended to adapt to the white man's way. As a result, they have been hounded and hunted out of the European areas, until today only a comparative few survive in the implacable wastes of the Kalahari Desert. They are short, a yellowish tan in color, and have left behind a legacy of art equalled by few African tribes.

These, then, are but a few of the many, fascinating peoples you will encounter on a trip through Africa. There are many more, and many more things to learn about those I have briefly described. If you but keep your eyes, ears, and heart open, you will be astounded at the new knowledge of human nature that will come your way.

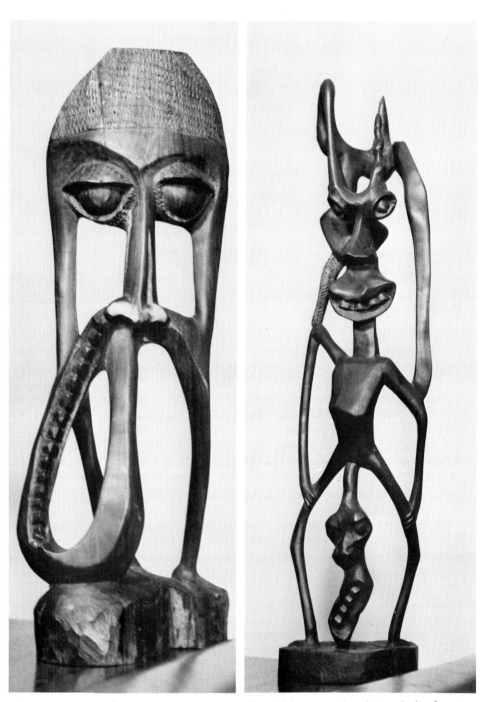

The weird and fanciful shapes of contemporary East African carved sculpture derive from two sources: the fact that many of the statues represent gods or devils; and the state of intoxication reached by the carvers after smoking some sort of local hallucinogen.

FOLLOW THE WEATHER

RULE ONE:

You must, of course, tour Africa when time and circumstances permit. You need only follow three rules. First: whenever you may plan to actually leave home, start now.

Many people spend their lives contemplating trips such as this, without ever leaving the comfort of their living rooms. If you wish to be one of the few who do what they dream about, make a commitment now. Get a passport; tell your friends; arrange for leave from your work. Once you get the ball rolling, you'll be amazed at how easy it all really is.

After twelve years of building a law practice, I quit cold and traveled for thirteen months. I regret not a moment of what turned out to be the most worthwhile enterprise of my life. Had I never taken that first step, almost by accident, I would still be dreaming about some day going to Africa.

TAKE ENOUGH TIME:

The second rule is: don't cheat yourself on time. Take an absolute minimum of six months for the full transcontinental trip. You could probably rush through it in four, but without really enjoying yourself. I spent seven, and feel that I should have stayed longer.

If you can wangle only a month or two, confine yourself to a limited objective. You could do East Africa comfortably in two months. A three weeks vacation isn't time enough to really see anything; but if that's all you've got, Nairobi is as pleasant a place to spend it as any.

DON'T BUCK THE WEATHER:

Touring Africa can be idyllic, miserable, or even impossible—depending almost entirely on the time of year. Rule three, if you have not already guessed, is to follow the good weather and avoid the bad.

Careful consultation of the chart appearing in the Appendix will keep you out of trouble. The Congo, for instance, is all but impassable during its March-to-November rainy season, the Sahara absolutely impassable during approximately the same period. East Africa is bearable, but not much fun, when it rains, mostly in March to May, perhaps again in November and December.

Also tricky are winter and summer. The equator passes through the heart of East Africa. Countries in this same latitude have no winter or summer— merely rainy and dry seasons. Those well above the equator, in northern Africa, have winter from November to February. Morocco, northern Algeria, and desert nights can be quite chilly. South Africa, Rhodesia, and other southern countries can be uncomfortably cold from June to August.

PICK A SCHEDULE, ANY SCHEDULE:

Following are two timetables, one heading south, the other north. Both will allow you to traverse the continent without encountering extremes of weather.

From north to south, try:

AREA	MONTH	COMMENT
North Africa	November	Not yet cold; not too hot
Trans-Sahara	December	Heat and sandstorms are at a minimum
Central Africa	January	Coolest month; no rain
East Africa	February	Between rainy seasons
South Africa	Mar.-Apr.	Not yet winter

Conversely, from south to north:

AREA	MONTH	COMMENT
South Africa	September	Winter's over
East Africa	Oct.-Nov.	Just before the light rainy season
Central Africa	December	Beginning of the dry weather
Trans-Sahara	January	Still cool and passable
North Africa	February	Winter's over; not hot yet

Arrange your own schedule if you prefer; but don't ignore that African weather.

122

IT'S CHEAPER THAN
STAYING
HOME

Aside from certain initial outlays, touring in Africa is far cheaper than remaining in the U.S. Your greatest expense, petrol, can be reduced considerably if you use diesel fuel. Food is cheap if you eat simply, hotels unnecessary if you have a camper. It is difficult to estimate what your expenses will be; I can only tell you what mine were.

My fixed expenses were as follows:

ITEM	PRICE	COMMENT
Investment in van	$300	Bought for $3,200; sold for $2,900
Air fare to Europe	200	You can get round trip for this amount
Camping equipment	100	Take it with you
Freight van home	850	Sell or abandon it at trip's end
Passage home	700	It's cheaper to fly
Total	$2,150	

Total running expenses, including petrol, food, repairs, maintenance, entertainment, and purchase of curios, for one person over seven months was another $1,700—under $250 per month.

I had little financial help with repairs and maintenance, and bought all my own fuel, oil, and tires for about half the trip. You should be able to undercut these items by sharing expenses. On the other hand, you couldn't eat and sleep much more cheaply. Native markets, grocery stores, and inexpensive restaurants for food, free camping for beddy bye. If you must live like an American, stay in hotels, and

Cape Town—the end of the long trek South.

eat in the best restaurants whenever possible, you'll spend a lot more—without having more fun.

You may be able to offset expenses, as I did, by letting out your house or apartment while gone. But demand a large security deposit before leaving, and authorize a nearby neighbor to evict or negotiate with the tenants. The damage may exceed the rent.

One other expense—you'll need a reserve to show border officials, and for emergencies. This can be in the form of travelers checks or letter of credit, as is pointed out in Chapter Nine. Say, one thousand to cover serious vehicular repairs, medical expenses, or other unforeseen contingencies. You won't want to run short in Agadez.

If you add it all up, you'll find it far cheaper than sitting at home, watching TV and eating from the local A&P.

APPENDIXES

APPENDIX I

CHART OF TRAVEL CONDITIONS BY NATION

NATION	LOCATION	LANGUAGE	CURRENCY	BLACK MARKET	VISA
Algeria	North - Sahara	French & Arabic	5 Dinars = $1.00	Yes - ratio unknown	Yes
Angola	Southwest	Portugese	28.75 Portugese Escudos = $1.00	Unknown	Yes
Botswana	South	English & Afrikaans	.714 South African Rand = $1.00	No	Not required
Burundi	East	French & Swahili	87.5 Francs = $1.00	Unknown	Yes - easy
Cameroun	West	French	277.7 Central African Francs = $1.00	No	Yes - easy
Central African Republic	Central	French	277.7 Central African Francs = $1.00	No	Yes - easy
Chad	Sahara	French	277.7 Central African Francs = $1.00	No	Yes - easy
Congo (Brazzaville)	Central	French	277.7 Central African Francs = $1.00	No	Yes
Congo (Kinshasha) /Zaire	Central	French	1 Zaire = $1.00	Yes - ratio unknown	Yes - difficult
Dahomey	West	French	277.7 Central African Francs = $1.00	No	Yes
Egypt /U.A.R.	North	Arabic	.44 Pounds = $1.00	Yes - exact ratio unknown	Yes
Equatorial Guinea	West	Spanish	70 Spanish Pestas = $1.00	No	Yes
Ethiopia	Northeast	Amharic, English & Arabic	1 Ethiopian Dollar = $1.00	Unknown	Yes
Gabon	Central	French	277.7 Central African Francs = $1.00	No	Yes
Gambia	West	English	2 Dalasi = $1.00	Unknown	Yes
Ghana	West	English	1 Cedi = $1.00	Unknown	Yes

126

DOCUMENTS	MEDICAL	ROADS	EQUIPMENT	SEASONS	COMMENTS
Carnet unnecessary	Desert: OK. Towns: watch food & water	34,000 paved miles North: smooth asphalt South: rough track	South: sand ladders, 4-wheel drive	Cold: Dec. - Jan.	Desert impassable: Mar. - Oct.
Civil war v. Portugal	Unknown	Unknown		Rain: Oct. - Apr.	Portugese colony
	Desert: OK. Towns: Unknown	Unpaved	Sand ladders, 4-wheel drive	Cold: Jun. - Aug.	Kalahari Desert
Native massacres, 1972	Unknown	50 paved miles			Tiny Republic between Congo & Uganda
Carnet or Temporary import permit	Watch out for everything - CHOLERA	7,000 "all weather" miles - mostly rock and gravel	None	Rain: Mar. - Nov.	Tropical & primitive
Carnet or temporary import permit	Watch out for everything	3,750 "all weather" miles - mostly rock and gravel	None	Rain: Mar. - Oct.	Tropical & primitive
	Desert: OK. Towns: Watch food & water	720 "all weather" miles - rough sand track	Sand ladders, 4-wheel drive	South: rain, May - Aug. (North: Desert)	Rough & expensive
Financial proof & police clearance	Watch out for everything	985 paved miles - rough rock & earth	Mud chains, 4-wheel drive	Impassable, rain: Oct. - Mar.	Tropical & primitive
Carnet a must - Financial & police clearance	Watch out for everything	1,000 "improved" miles - Horrible rock & gravel	Mud chains 4-wheel drive	Impassable, rain: Mar. - Nov.	Tropical & primitive. No entry after Congo (Brazzaville)
	Watch out for everything	Only 400 paved miles	None	Rain: Mar. - Oct.	Primitive, tropical & Poor
War w/ Israel; attempted coup, 1971.	Desert: OK. Towns: watch food & water	6,500 paved miles. Touring by auto prohibited		Cold: Dec. - Jan.	Home of Sphinx, Pyramid, Nile. No entry after Israel
		Only 94 paved miles		Rain: Sep. - May	Tiny country between Cameroun & Gabon
Rebellion, 1971.		1,100 paved miles		Semi-impassable, rain: Mar. - Sep.	Home of ancient African culture
	Watch out for everything	3,000 paved miles		Rain: Sep. - May	Tropical jungle. Poor
		Only 173 paved miles		Rain: Jun. - Oct.	Tiny strip of land surrounded by Senegal. Recent tourist resort.
		21,000 "highway" miles		Rain: Mar. - Oct.	Progressive, agricultural State. Jungle & plains.

NATION	LOCATION	LANGUAGE	CURRENCY	BLACK MARKET	VISA
Guinea	West	French	247 Francs = $1.00	Unknown	Yes
Ivory Coast	West	French	277.7 Central African Francs = $1.00	No	Yes
Kenya	East	English & Swahili	7.14 Shillings = $1.00	Yes - 9 to 1	Yes - easy
Lesotho	South	English	.714 South African Rand = $1.00	No	Not required
Liberia	West	English	U.S. Dollars	No	Yes
Libya	North	Arabic, English, & Italian	1 Pound = $3.00	Unknown	Yes
Malagasay Republic (Madagascar)	Southeast (island)	French & Malagasay	277.7 Francs = $1.00	Unknown	Yes
Malawi	South	English	.714 Kwacha = $1.00	No	Yes
Mali	Sahara	French	555 Francs = $1.00	Unknown	Yes
Mauritania	West - Sahara	French & Arabic	277.7 Central African Francs = $1.00	No	Yes
Morocco	North	French & Arabic	5 Dirham = $1.00	No	Not required
Mozambique	Southeast	Portugese	28.75 Portugese Escudos = $1.00	No	Yes - easy
Niger	Sahara	French	277.7 Central African Francs = $1.00	No	Yes - easy
Nigeria	West	English	7.14 Shillings = $1.00	Yes - 12 to 1	Yes - very difficult
Portugese Guinea	West	Portugese	28.75 Portugese Escudos = $1.00	No	Yes
Rhodesia	South	English	.714 Rhodesian Dollars = $1.00	No	Not required

DOCUMENTS	MEDICAL	ROADS	EQUIPMENT	SEASONS	COMMENTS
	Watch out for everything	8,000 paved miles		Rain: May - Oct.	Poor. Varied country
	Watch out for everything	Only 745 paved miles		Rain: Mar. - Dec.	Prosperous & progressive
Carnet required	Food & water OK. Watch out for insects.	20,000 paved miles. Good asphalt & earth	None	Rain: Mar. - May & Nov. - Dec.	The original Garden of Eden. Easy traveling. Don't miss it
		1,338 paved miles		Cold: Jun. - Aug.	Pocket-sized Kingdom surrounded by South Africa
	Rain: Apr. - Dec.	1,200 paved miles		Rain: Apr. - Dec.	Progressive country founded by freed U.S. slaves
	Desert: OK. Towns: Watch food & water	1 paved road. Balance sand track	Sand ladders, 4-wheel drive	Cold: Nov. - Jan.	Mostly desert
Attempted coup, 1971.		1243 paved miles	None	Rain: Nov. - Mar.	Large island 250 miles from Southeast Africa
Carnet required.	Can swim in Lake Malawi.	288 paved miles. Mostly good rock & gravel	None	Rain: Nov. - Mar.	Delightful scenery, pleasant people, good touring
	Desert: OK. Towns: watch food & water	4,600 paved miles. Lots of sand track	Sand ladders, 4-wheel drive	Rain: North, Jul. - Aug.; South: Jun. - Sep.	Timbuktu & desert
Financial proof	Desert: OK. Towns: watch food & water	All sand track	Sand ladders, 4-wheel drive	No rain, no winter	Mostly desert
Carnet not required. Long hair touchy. Attempted coup, 1971.	Food & water chancy	11,200 paved miles. Mostly smooth asphalt. Donkey-cart traffic.	None	Cold, rain: Dec. - Jan.	Interesting & easy to visit
Carnet not required. Civil war v. Portugal.	Watch out for everything	Earth & gravel. Rough in rain.	Mud chains, 4-wheel drive	Rain: Nov. - Mar.	Primitive & poor
Carnet not required	Desert: OK. Towns & South: watch out	Dirt roads & sand track. Rough	Sand ladders, 4-wheel drive	Rain: South, Jun. - Sep; North, none	Mostly desert
Carnet or bribery required	Watch out for everything	9,500 paved miles. North: good asphalt, heavy traffic	None	Rain: North, May - Aug.; South, Mar. - Nov.	Very crowded. Friendly natives. Very difficult border
	Watch out for everything	Mostly unpaved		Rain: Jun. - Oct.	Hot & wet
Financial proof	No problems	3,400 paved miles. Good gravel & strip roads	None	Rain: Nov. - Mar. Cold: Jun. - Aug.	Little South Africa. Civilized & anti-black

NATION	LOCATION	LANGUAGE	CURRENCY	BLACK MARKET	VISA
Rwanda	East	French	100 Francs = $1.00	Unknown	Yes - easy
Senegal	West	French	277.7 Central African Francs = $1.00	No	Yes
Sierra Leone	West	English	1 Leone = $1.20	Unknown	Yes
Somalia	East	Arabic, English & Italian	7.14 Shillings = $1.00	Unknown	Yes
South Africa	South	English & Afrikaans	.714 Rand = $1.00	No	Yes
South West Africa (Namibia)	South	English & Afrikaans	.714 South African Rand = $1.00	No	Visa & carnet unnecessary if coming from South Africa
Spanish Sahara	North - West	Spanish	70 Spanish Pesetas = $1.00	No	
Sudan	Northeast	Arabic, French & English	1 Pound = $3.00	Unknown	Yes
Swaziland	South	Swazi & English	.714 South African Rand = $1.00	No	Not required
Tanzania	East	English & Swahili	7.14 Shillings = $1.00	Too dangerous	Yes - easy
Togo	West	French	277.7 Central African Francs = $1.00	No	Yes
Tunisia	North	French & Arabic	1 Dinar = $2.00	Unknown	Not required
Uganda	East	English	7.14 Shillings = $1.00	Yes - 10 to 1	Yes - easy
Upper Volta	West	French	277.7 Central African Francs = $1.00	No	Yes
Zambia	South- Central	English	.714 Kwacha = $1.00	Unknown	Yes - easy

DOCUMENTS	MEDICAL	ROADS	EQUIPMENT	SEASONS	COMMENTS
		3,400 paved miles.			Scenic home of the lofty Watusi. Tiny country
	Watch out for everything	2,600 paved miles.		Rain: Jun. - Oct.	Steppe desert & savannah
oups in '67, 68, & '71		1,400 paved miles		Rain: May - Oct.	Progressive, shaky government
oups in '69 '70	Desert: OK. Towns: watch food & water	Unpaved		Rain: North, none; South, Apr. - Aug.	Largely desert & arid mountains
inancial roof. Carnet must	No problems	116,000 paved miles. Best roads in Africa. Almost all paved	None	Rain: Nov. - Mar. Cold: Jun. - Aug.	Much like America. Apartheid & concrete
	No problems	Mostly good, paved roads. Some desert track	None	Cold: Jun. - Aug. Little rain	Mostly desert. Ruled by South Africa
	Desert: OK. Towns: watch food & water	Rough sand track	Sand ladders, 4-wheel drive	Little rain or cold	Largely desert
lay prohibit ntry. Civil war coups in '71.	Desert: OK. Towns: watch food & water	200 paved miles. Lots of rough track	Sand ladders, 4-wheel drive	Rain, impassable: South, Jun. - Aug.; North, none	Largest African nation. Desert in North, Central plains, Southern swamp
		100 paved miles		Rain: Oct. - Mar. Cold: Jun. - Aug.	Pocket kingdom surrounded by South Africa
arnet required. oreign commercial ehicle tax. War w/ ganda in '72.	Food & water OK. Watch out for insects	3,000 paved miles. Mostly rock & earth. Hell Run into Zambia	None	Rain: Mar. - May, Nov. - Dec.	Home of Serengeti & Kilimanjaro
	Watch out for everything	3,000 paved miles		Rain: Mar. - Oct.	Small country supported by markets, trade & smuggling
	Desert: OK. Towns: watch food & water	10,000 paved miles.	None	Cold, rain: Nov. - Jan.	Most progressive & stable of Arab nations
arnet required. oup in '71. War / Tanzania in '72.	Food & water OK. Watch out for insects	24,000 paved miles. Some good earth roads	None	Rain: Mar. - May, Nov. - Dec.	Scenic Mountains of the Moon. Good game parks.
	Watch out for everything	10,000 paved miles		Rain: May - Dec.	Poor, landlocked, agricultural country
arnet required		800 paved miles		Rain: Nov. - Apr.	Victoria Falls & copper mines

Appendix II

CHART OF ROADS TRAVELED BY AUTHOR

NATION	FROM	TO	ROAD MATERIAL	TOP SPEED
Morocco	Ceuta	Tangier	Asphalt	60
Morocco	Tangier	Rabat	Asphalt	60
Morocco	Rabat	Casablanca	Asphalt	60
Morocco	Rabat	Fez	Asphalt	60
Morocco	Fez	Tangier	Asphalt	60
Morocco	Tangier	Oujda	Broken asphalt	40
Morocco	Oujda	Figuig	Asphalt	60
Algeria	Figuig	Bechar	Asphalt	60
Algeria	Bechar	Adrar	Asphalt	60
Algeria	Adrar	Reggane	Sand	40
Algeria	Reggane	In Salah	Sand	40
Algeria	In Salah	Tamanrasset	Sand & rock	45
Algeria	Tamanrasset	Assamaka	Sand & rock	45
Niger	Assamaka	Agadez	Loose sand	45
Niger	Agadez	Zinder	Loose sand	35
Niger	Zinder	Maradi	Smooth dirt	40
Niger/ Nigeria	Maradi	Kano	Asphalt	50
Nigeria	Kano	Maiduguri	Asphalt	50
Nigeria	Maiduguri	Bama	Asphalt	50
Nigeria	Bama	Maroua	Dirt & rock	35
Cameroun				
Cameroun	Maroua	Ngaoundere	Earth & asphalt	45
Cameroun	Ngaoundere	Garoua-Boulai	Earth	45
Cameroun	Garoua-Boulai	Bertoua	Earth	45
Cameroun	Bertoua	Yaounde	Earth	45
Cameroun	Yaounde	Edea	Earth	45

MILES	TIME	SEASONAL PROBLEMS	COMMENTS
58	1 hour	No sweat	Smooth & easy
177	3 hours	No sweat	Smooth & easy
58	1 hour	No sweat	Smooth & easy
123	2¼ hours	No sweat	Smooth & easy
200 (est.)	4 hours	No sweat	Smooth & easy
379	12 hours	Rough in rain (Dec. - Jan.)	Rough, mountain road; rocks and potholes
233	5 hours	No sweat	Smooth & easy
71	1¼ hours	No sweat	Smooth & easy
373	1 day	No sweat	Smooth & easy
86	½ day	Impassable Jun. - Oct.	Rough washboard; drifting sand; potholes. Tough
178	1 day	Impassable Jun. - Oct.	Rough washboard; drifting sand; potholes. Tough
430	2 days	Impassable Jun. - Oct.	Washboard; rock; sand. But driveable
200 (est.)	1 day	Impassable Jun. - Oct.	Washboard; rock; sand. But driveable
240 (est.)	2 days	Impassable Jun. - Oct.	Badly marked; loose sand; tough
293	2 days	Impassable Jun. - Oct.	Deep sand; toughest desert stretch; avoid it
147	4 hours	Rough in rain (Nov. - Mar.)	Good dirt road when dry
140	3½ hours	No sweat	Narrow asphalt; heavy traffic; be careful
377	1½ days	No sweat	Good asphalt, w/detours; part expressway
43	1 hour	No sweat	Good asphalt
60 (est.)	2 hours	Rough in rain (Jun. - Sep.)	Lousy earth road; bad potholes
306 (est.)	1 day	Rough in rain (Mar. - Nov.)	Fair rock & dirt road; potholes
166	½ day	Rough in rain (Mar. - Nov.)	Fair rock & dirt road; potholes
166	½ day	Rough in rain (Mar. - Nov.)	Fair rock & dirt road; potholes
214	6 hours	Rough in rain (Mar. - Nov.)	Fair rock & dirt road; potholes
110 (est.)	3 hours	Rough in rain (Mar. - Nov.)	Fair rock & dirt road; potholes

NATION	FROM	TO	ROAD MATERIAL	TOP SPEED
Cameroun	Edea	Kribi	Earth	40
Cameroun	Edea	Douala	Asphalt	55
Cameroun	Douala	Victoria	Earth	45
Cameroun/ R.C.A.	Garoua-Boulai	Bangui	Earth	40
R.C.A.	Bangui	Sibut	Asphalt & earth	50
R.C.A.	Sibut	Bangassou	Earth	40
Congo (K.)	Bangassou	Buta	Earth	35
Congo (K.)	Buta	Isiro	Earth	25
Congo (K.)	Isiro	Wamba	Earth	35
Congo (K.)	Wamba	Mungbere	Earth	20
Congo (K.)	Mungbere	Mambasa	Smooth gravel	45
Congo (K.)	Mambasa	Beni	Earth	10
Congo (K.)/ Uganda	Beni	Queen Elizabeth Park	Earth	35
Uganda	Queen Elizabeth Park	Fort Portal	Asphalt	65
Uganda	Queen Elizabeth Park	Ishasha	Asphalt & gravel	55
Uganda	Queen Elizabeth Park	Kabale	Asphalt	55
Uganda	Fort Portal	Semiliki Reserve	Asphalt & gravel	45
Uganda	Fort Portal	Kampala	Gravel	40
Uganda	Kampala	Gulu	Asphalt	70
Uganda	Gulu	Soroti	Earth	35
Uganda	Soroti	Tororo	Asphalt	55
Kenya	Tororo	Nairobi	Asphalt	60
Kenya	Nairobi	Nanyuki	Asphalt	65
Kenya	Nairobi	Mombasa	Asphalt & earth	60
Kenya	Mombasa	Malindi	Asphalt	55
Kenya/ Tanzania	Voi	Moshi	Earth & asphalt	40

MILES	TIME	SEASONAL PROBLEMS	COMMENT
57 (est.)	1½ hours	Rough in rain (Mar. - Nov.)	Better rock road; part maintained by huge plantation
62 (est.)	1¼ hours	No sweat	Fair-to-good asphalt road
33 (est.)	1 hour	Rough in rain (Mar. - Nov.)	Fair rock & dirt road; potholes
382	2 days	Rough in rain (Mar. - Oct.)	Bad dirt & rock road; nasty potholes
115	2½ hours	No sweat	Asphalt & very good rock road
249	1 day	Rough in rain (Mar. - Oct.)	Very good rock road; last 60 miles rough
241	1 day	Rough in rain (Mar. - Nov.)	Poor earth road; narrow; holes & bumps
284	1½ days	Rough in rain (Mar. - Nov.)	Lousy earth track
76 (est.)	2½ hours	Rough in rain (Mar. - Nov.)	Fair earth track
65 (est.)	4 hours	Impassable in rain (Mar. - Nov.)	Horrible, rutted earth track; avoid it
121	3 hours	No sweat	Good gravel road; best in the Congo
86	1 day	Impassable in rain (Mar. - Nov.)	Godawful; worst of entire trip; don't try it
74	2½ hours	Rough in rain (Mar. - Nov.)	Bad earth track
69	1¼ hours	No sweat	Fine, asphalt road
102	2 hours	No sweat	Good road, but not a highway
150	3 hours	No sweat	Nice, paved road
50	1½ hours	No sweat	Paved mountain road; some gravel; scenic
198	5 hours	Rough in rain (Mar.-May,Nov.-Dec.)	Rough, gravel road; potholes; washboard
210	3 hours	No sweat	Modern, paved, 2-lane highway
144	4 hours	Rough in rain (Mar.-May, Nov.-Dec.)	Bad, rough, potholed, earth road
91	2 hours	No sweat	Good, paved road
283	6 hours	No sweat	Good, paved road; climb up & down escarpment slow
118 (est.)	3 hours	No sweat	Paved, modern highway
306	1 day	No real problem	Good, paved road, w/ rough, gravel detours
75	2 hours	No sweat	Fair-to-good, paved road
93	2½ hours	Rough in rain (Mar.-May, Nov.-Dec.)	Fairly good earth road w/some asphalt

NATION	FROM	TO	ROAD MATERIAL	TOP SPEED
Tanzania	Moshi	Makuyuni	Asphalt	60
Tanzania	Makuyuni	Serengeti Park	Earth & gravel	45
Tanzania	Moshi	Dar Es Salaam	Asphalt & dirt detours	60
Tanzania	Dar Es Salaam	Mbeya	Asphalt & earth	50
Tanzania/Zambia /Malawi	Mbeya	Chitipa	Earth & asphalt	45
Malawi	Chitipa	Karonga	Gravel	45
Malawi	Karonga	Nkhata Bay	Gravel	45
Malawi	Nkhata Bay	Lilongwe	Gravel	45
Malawi	Lilongwe	Blantyre	Gravel & asphalt	55
Malawi/Mozam- bique/Rhodesia	Blantyre	Mtoko	Earth & gravel	45
Rhodesia	Mtoko	Salisbury	Asphalt & earth	55
Rhodesia	Salisbury	Fort Victoria	Asphalt	65
Rhodesia	Fort Victoria	Zimbabwe	Strip	45
Rhodesia	Fort Victoria	Bulawayo	Asphalt	65
Rhodesia/ South Africa	Bulawayo	Louis Trichardt	Asphalt	65
South Africa	Louis Trichardt	Kruger Park	Asphalt	60
South Africa	Kruger Park	Nelspruit	Asphalt	55
South Africa	Nelspruit	Pretoria	Asphalt	65
South Africa	Pretoria	Johannesburg	Asphalt	70
South Africa	Johannesburg	Ladysmith	Asphalt	65
South Africa	Ladysmith	Durban	Asphalt	65
South Africa	Durban	East London	Asphalt	65
South Africa	East London	Port Elizabeth	Asphalt	65
South Africa	Port Elizabeth	Swellandam	Asphalt	65
South Africa	Swellandam	Worcester	Asphalt	65
South Africa	Worcester	Cape Town	Asphalt	65
South Africa	Cape Town	Springbok	Asphalt	70
South Africa/ South West Africa	Sprinbok	Keetmanshoop	Asphalt	70
South West Africa	Keetmanshoop	Windhoek	Asphalt	70
South West Africa	Windhoek	Okanandja	Asphalt	70
South West Africa	Okanandja	Walvis Bay	Earth	40

MILES	TIME	SEASONAL PROBLEMS	COMMENT
110	2¼ hours	No sweat	Good, paved road
100 (est.)	4 hours	Rough in rain (Mar.-May, Nov.-Dec.)	Ngorongoro a sea of mud when wet; otherwise OK
331	1 day	Rough in rain . (Mar.-May, Nov.-Dec.)	Asphalt fine; detours muddy & rough in wet
556	2 days	Rough all year	Mud; dust; potholes; good asphalt being built; Hell Run—well named
128	3 hours	Rough in rain (Mar.-May, Nov.-Dec.)	Fair gravel, earth, some asphalt
78	2 hours	No sweat	Good gravel road
223	1 day	Rough in rain (Nov. - Mar.)	Fair gravel; climb up Livingston escarpment tough
309	1 day	Rough in rain (Nov. - Mar.)	Fair-to-good gravel
222	1 day	Rough in rain (Nov. - Mar.)	Fair-to-good gravel & some asphalt
306 (est.)	1 day	Rough in rain (Nov. - Mar.)	Fair gravel & earth; potholes
100 (est.)	2 hours	No sweat	Good gravel; last few miles paved
187	3 hours	No sweat	Fine, paved road
30 (est.)	1 hour	No sweat	2 narrow strips of asphalt; quite adequate
181 (est.)	3½ hours	No sweat	Good, paved road
270	5 hours	No sweat	Fine, paved highway
100 (est.)	2 hours	No sweat	Good, paved road
35 (est.)	1 hour	No sweat	Good, paved road
219	4 hours	No sweat	Fine, paved highway
35	½ hour	No sweat	Fine, paved highway
195	3½ hours	No sweat	Fine, paved road
156	3 hours	No sweat	Fine, paved road
421	1½ days	No sweat	Fine, paved road
197	½ day	No sweat	Fine, paved road
380	1 day	No sweat	Fine, paved road
69	1½ hours	No sweat	Fine, paved road
78	1½ hours	No sweat	Fine, paved road
369	1 day	No sweat	Fine, paved road
283	1 day	No sweat	Fine, paved road
316	1 day	No sweat	Fine, paved road
45	1 hour	No sweat	Fine, paved road
219	5½ hours	Rough all year	Fair, earth track; potholes

APPENDIX IV
METRIC AND BRITISH CONVERSIONS

DISTANCE:

1 inch = 25.4 millimeters (5 = 127)
1 foot = .3048 meters (292 = 89)
1 yard = .9144 meters (35 = 32)
1 mile = 1.6093 kilometers (87 = 140)
1 mile = 1609.3472 meters

1 millimeter = .03937 inches (127 = 5)
1 meter = 39.37 inches
1 meter = 3.2808 feet
1 meter = 1.0936 yards (32 = 35)
1 kilometer = 1093.6 yards
1 kilometer = .62137 miles (approximately 5/8)

CAPACITY:

1 imperial gallon = 1.2001 U.S. gallon (5 = 6)
1 imperial gallon = 4.546 liters (308 = 1400)
1 U.S. gallon = 3.7853 liters (37 = 140)

1 liter = 1.0567 U.S. quarts
1 liter = .26418 U.S. gallon (1400 = 308)

SPEED:

1 mile per hour = 1.6093 kilometers per hour
1 kilometer per hour = .62137 miles per hour

CONSUMPTION:

1 U.S. gallon per mile = 2.3521 liters per kilometer

TEMPERATURE:

Degrees Centigrade = (Degrees Fahrenheit - 32) x 5/9
Degrees Fahrenheit = (Degrees Centigrade x 9/5) + 32

APPENDIX V
NAMES AND ADDRESSES

AUTOMOTIVE:

British Leyland Motors, 600 Willow Tree Road, Leonia, New Jersey 07605
Dormobile, Ltd., Folkestone, Kent, England
Motion Minicar Corp., 594 Sunrise Highway, Baldwin, New York 11510
Customer Relations, Volkswagen of America, Englewood Cliffs, New Jersey 07632
Warshawsky & Company, 1900 South State Street, Chicago, Illinois 60616
J. C. Whitney & Company, 1917 Archer Avenue, Chicago, Illinois 60616

BOOKS AND MAPS:

Arizona Ordnance Company, P.O. Box 20191, Phoenix, Arizona 85036
Henry Elfrink Automotive, P.O. Box 20367, Los Angeles, California 90006
Merck, Sharp and Dohme Research Laboratories, Professional Service Department,
    West Point,   Pennsylvania 19486
Michelin Tyre Company, Ltd., 81, Fullham Road, London, S.W. 3, England
Pneu Michelin, Services de Tourisme, 97 Bd. Pereire, Paris, 17, France
R. W. Simpson & Company, Ltd., 70, Sheen Road, Richmond, Surrey, England
Thornton Cox, 3 Colebrook Court, Sloane Avenue, London, S.W. 3, England
U.S. Government Printing Office, Washington, D.C. 20402
Warshawsky & Company, 1900 South State Street, Chicago, Illinois 60616
J. C. Whitney & Company, 1917 Archer Avenue, Chicago, Illinois 60616

CAMPING GEAR:

Arthur Ellis and Company, Private Bag, Dunedin, New Zealand
Camel, 329 South Central Street, Knoxville, Tennessee 37902
Gander Mountain Inc., Wilmot, Wisconsin 53192
Klein's, 227 West Washington Street, Chicago, Illinois 60606
L. L. Bean, Freeport, Maine 04032
Recreational Equipment, Inc., 1525 11th Avenue, Seattle, Washington 98122

INSURANCE:

American Home Assurance Company, 102 Maiden Lane, New York, New York 10005
American International Underwriters, 2355 South Salzedo Street, Coral Gables, Florida 33134
Firemen's Insurance Company of Newark, New Jersey, 102 Maiden Lane, New York, New York
    10005

APPENDIX VI

CHECKLISTS

BOOKS AND MAPS:

Africa on Wheels
Africa Center and South, Michelin Map Number 155
Africa North and East, Michelin Map Number 154
Africa North and West, Michelin Map Number 153
Modern Home Medical Adviser
The Merck Manual
Travellers' Guide to East Africa
Upcountry Swahili
French and Afrikaans dictionaries and grammars
repair and service manuals for your vehicle

CLOTHING:

1 sportcoat
1 tie
2 short-sleeve sport shirts
3 T-shirts
1 wool shirt
1 wool sweater
2 semi-dressy jeans
1 casual slacks
2 short pants
2 undershorts
1 heavy jacket
1 windbreaker
1 rainsuit

2 belts, 1 dressy, 1 rough
2 heavy wool sox
3 lighter sox
rubber shower clogs
waterproof hiking boots
combination sneakers-casual-dress shoes
swim trunks
clothesline & clothespins
1 sunhat
2 sunglasses
1 towel
1 washcloth

sewing kit: thread, black, white, and brown
pack of assorted needles
pack of carpet and upholstery needles
thimble
straight pins
safety pins
scissors
razor blade

DISEASE PREVENTION:

Before setting out:	cholera shots smallpox vaccination typhoid-paratyphoid shots yellow fever inoculation assemble medical kit
In North, West, or Central Africa:	purify all drinking water protect food from flies peel or cook all fresh foods wash hands before handling food wash hands after defecating
Anywhere in Africa:	take malaria pills as directed use mosquito netting use Off and Raid watch where you step don't touch still, fresh water clean and drain all wounds see a doctor promptly if exposed

DOCUMENTS:

carnet du passage in douane
certificate of title to motor vehicle
health certificate ("shot card")
insurance certificate ("green card")

international driver's license
passport
registration of motor vehicle
student card (optional)

FIRST AID KIT:

variegated band aids
first aid cream or disinfectant
tincture of iodine
gauze pads
adhesive tape
scissors
vaseline or unguentine
eyewash with cup
snakebite kit
polyvalent antivenins
malaria suppression tablets
enterovioform
aspirin
pain pills

nose drops
cough medicine
alcohol
halazone tablets
elastic bandages
sunburn lotion
Off and Raid
tourniquet
razor blade
splinting materials
first aid book
Africa on Wheels
personal prescriptions

KITCHEN UTENSILS:

coffeepot
pots, with lids, large and small
frying pan
coffee cups
knives, forks, spoons
kitchen or bread knife
whetstone
dinner plates
cutting board

spatula
salt and pepper shakers
water bottles
can and bottle openers
small sponges
dishwashing detergent
scouring powder
Brillo

SPARE PARTS:

oil, one gallon
grease, one pound
2 spare tires, mounted
2 extra tires (optional)
2 extra tubes
tire patching kit
mud chains (optional)
radiator stop-leak
radiator hoses
hot-water-heater plugs
epoxy or aircraft adhesive
cool cushions
set of points
set of plugs
distributor rotor
distributor cap
condenser
fanbelt
extra battery (optional)
electrical wire
baling wire
assorted nuts, bolts, sheet-metal screws
clutch disc
assorted gaskets
flashlight bulbs and batteries

TOOLS:

feeler gauge set

wirecutters and crimper

pocket knife

socket set

sparkplug socket

open end wrench set

large crescent wrench

pliers, channel locks, or vise grips

screwdrivers, standard and phillips, large and small

siphon hose

heavy hammer

grease gun

funnel or pouring spout, with strainer

gas cans

water cans

towrope

shovel

machete or hatchet

sand ladders

foot pump

2 tire irons

2 jacks

jack base

lug wrench

tire gauge

hacksaw

files

fire extinguisher

jumper cables

flashlight

service and repair manuals

coveralls (optional)

ground sheet (optional)

WEATHER:

North-to-South schedule:	North Africa: November
	Trans-Sahara: December
	Central Africa: January
	East Africa: February
	South Africa: March to April
South-to-North schedule:	South Africa: September
	East Africa: October to November
	Central Africa: December
	Trans-Sahara: January
	North Africa: February to March

INDEX

152